IMAGES
of America

FOREST GLEN

This 1887 watercolor shows the newly completed Ye Forest Inne in Forest Glen, Maryland. Designed by famed Washington, D.C. architect Thomas Franklin Schneider, the inn was built for the Forest Glen Improvement Company by the George Lipscomb Construction Company for just under $100,000. Its purpose, though short-lived, was to lure city dwellers out of Washington to the clean, healthy, and easily accessible suburbs of Montgomery County, Maryland, to build new homes. Although a short trip by railroad from D.C., the hotel encouraged little new home development but many weekend and overnight respites, especially when the owners added gambling and alcohol as a last-ditch effort to keep the inn afloat and the investors out of bankruptcy. Fortunately, a couple from Norfolk bought the rustic inn and opened a fashionable girl's school in 1894. Today, the building stands and will soon again be the nucleus and glory of Forest Glen.

IMAGES
of America

FOREST GLEN

Rich Schaffer and Ric Nelson

ARCADIA
PUBLISHING

Published by Arcadia Publishing
Charleston SC, Chicago IL, Portsmouth NH, San Francisco CA

Library of Congress Catalog Card Number: 2004108733

For all general information contact Arcadia Publishing at:
Telephone 843-853-2070
Fax 843-853-0044
E-mail sales@arcadiapublishing.com
For customer service and orders:
Toll-Free 1-888-313-2665

Visit us on the Internet at www.arcadiapublishing.com

CONTENTS

ACKNOWLEDGMENTS

Rich Schaffer and Ric Nelson, authors of *Forest Glen* and both longtime historians and residents, have written this story based on years of personal research, interaction on the site, and oral interviews conducted between 1944 and 2004. Photographs appearing within are from our personal collection, which include a large number of annuals and scrapbooks. We wish to thank all those who made the Forest Glen story possible. Although the list is quite long, we have acknowledged those we feel were most critical in creating and insuring the story of Forest Glen: the lost and often forgotten legacy of the Carrolls of Rock Creek, who truly were the first residents of Forest Glen and for whom we are so proud to claim as our own; the early and long lost plantations of Edgewood and Highlands; the freedmen and their families, who set up the tiny and all but decimated community of Lyttonsville; the Forest Glen Improvement Company, who recognized the rustic beauty of the woods and its deep glens and thereby worked hard to create an idyllic neighborhood that is today our community; the vision of John and Vesta Cassedy (predecessors to James Eli Ament and Roy Tasco Davis), who established and maintained the architectural jewel of the region and an institution that catered to refining young women and later to the women's movement itself; the United States Army, who for 40 years here tirelessly cared for recuperating soldiers who fought bravely for our democracy and freedom; Save Our Seminary Inc., who twice prevented demolition of the historic district and worked feverishly for 15 years to guide its future and interpret its history; the memory of local historian Edith Ray Saul, who defined historical creed in the lower county and, whilst a Kensingtonite, always knew her origins were in Forest Glen and was proud to say her grandmother gave us the name; and The Alexander Company, who has undertaken revitalization and a new beginning for Forest Glen.

These are but a few of the many hundreds of people who over the past two centuries have lived, loved, and learned in the deep green woods of Forest Glen. To them, this book is dedicated.

INTRODUCTION

The first settlers in what is now Forest Glen, other than the indigenous Algonquin-speaking Piscataway Indians, were tenant tobacco farmers who lived in the area after 1736. Known then as Joseph's Park, the area had been part of a 4,220-acre land grant to William Joseph a half-century prior. That same year, much of the grant was purchased by Daniel Carroll of Upper Marlboro, Maryland. He passed away in 1750, leaving a wife, four daughters, and two sons. The widow, Eleanor Darnall Carroll, moved to the area the following year. Mrs. Carroll, who by every means deserves sainthood, established not only a fine home, but also a legacy that helped build a nation. Perhaps also, it should be understood this family did not build Forest Glen. They most likely came here because they wanted seclusion as they were practicing Catholicism when it was not allowed. This may also stand to reason why there is little historical record of the house. The Carrolls were a fixture in Joseph's Park for over a century, prospered, and went on to greater things.

Mrs. Carroll was a fairly wealthy widow, and to say the family lived on income from their tobacco crop in Joseph's Park is a misnomer, as records of the families farming activity here are moot. Records do show as many as 50 slaves who worked in and around the house, but no records indicate any working in substantial fields. It is very likely Mrs. Carroll lived comfortably on leasing and selling the vast land holdings her husband and her family had previously acquired, and they most likely never did more than domestic farming on the Joseph's Park property. However, despite leading a fairly comfortable life in the woods of what later became Forest Glen, the return of Mrs. Carroll's sons, John and Daniel, from schooling abroad found her tirelessly supporting her sons' endeavors and encouraging their many achievements.

How the name Rock Creek was established for this region prior to it being named Forest Glen is a bit of a mystery. It could have been adopted about the time John Carroll established his parish, which served an area abounded by Rock Creek, or it could have been the Carrolls' close proximity to the creek and its many tributaries on their property that influenced the name. The Carrolls' use of the name Rock Creek seems a bit more prevalent after John's ordination, so the former seems more likely. Both John and Daniel were given titles "of Rock Creek." The name Forest Glen came into being sometime between 1873 and 1887 when the wife of Alfred Ray was asked what she thought would be an appropriate name for the railroad station to serve her husband's property, the Highlands. Inspired by the heavy forests and deep bifurcated glen, her response was "Forest Glen." When the Metropolitan Branch of the Baltimore and Ohio Railroad built a full-service passenger station there in 1887, the name became official. From that day, the story of Forest Glen begins, and what happened lends credence to the philosophy that if the purpose of architecture is to give dignified stance to human life, Forest Glen is the utopia of existence.

One

STRONG IN FAITH AND WAR

Eleanor Carroll's Rock Creek home was built in 1751 after she moved from Upper Marlboro, Maryland. It may have stood in today's 2400 block of Seminary Road. Margaret Brent Downing, in her essay "The Development of the Catholic Church in the District of Columbia from Colonial Times Until the Present," claims the mansion burned down before 1911. However, historian Mildred Getty, who grew up around the site, believed this to be the original, which was burned for new housing development in 1953. A large center chimney, the four exterior chimneys with corbelled caps, and the long, narrow windows suggest the age of the home, here shadowed and misplaced by Victorian additions, a porch, and a new mansard roof. (Photo by Gail Hill.)

Many tribes in this region were nomadic "hunters and gatherers" and moved quite regularly around the Piedmont and Bay area. Many lived near Rock Creek and took advantage of abundant fish and wildlife. This sketch, titled "Indian Town Secotan," depicts a location near Roanoke Island, North Carolina, and was drawn in 1585 by John White. (Library of Congress.)

Eleanor Darnall (1703–1796) married Daniel Carroll of Upper Marlboro in 1727 and had eight children; one son died as an infant and another drowned as a youth. Their son John essentially began Catholicism in the United States, first in his mother's home and then on his mother's land in the first Catholic chapel under secular clergy. Another son Daniel lived life as a country gentleman with his family's wealth and focused on the developing nation, later participating in creating our fledgling government. Daughters Elizabeth (who did not marry and lived chiefly with her mother), Ann, Mary, and Eleanor kept ties to the area and had homes here. Mrs. Carroll is buried at St. Johns Forest Glen. (Painting by John Wallaston, John Carroll University.)

Born in 1735, John Carroll was schooled abroad, attending a Jesuit school and studying liberal arts at Saint Omer's College in French Flanders. In 1753, John joined the Society of Jesus and two years later began studying theology. Ordained a priest in 1769, he taught for many years in Europe. Upon returning to Rock Creek in 1773, he found Catholicism banned and began holding services in his mother's home and then in a nearby chapel. A close friend of such patriots as George Washington, he accompanied Benjamin Franklin and Samuel Chase in 1776 to Canada to impress neutrality upon them prior to the Revolution. After the war, he moved to Baltimore and was appointed bishop in 1789. He founded Georgetown College in 1791 and was appointed archbishop in 1808. He died in 1815 and is buried in Baltimore. (Portrait by Gilbert Stewart, Georgetown University.)

Born in 1733, Daniel Carroll was politically one of the most influential men in the United States. Educated beyond normal scholastics of the time, Daniel later lived in Rock Creek. His education led him to interests beyond the homestead, and he did much for the developing nation. Daniel became an active partisan of the colonies, serving in the Maryland legislature from 1777 to 1781 and as a Maryland member of the Continental Congress from 1781 to 1784. He signed the Articles of Confederation and the Constitution and was chosen by his friend George Washington to survey the location for the new capital. He laid the city's first boundary-stone in 1791. Daniel passed away in 1796 at Rock Creek, and the authors conclude his grave to be in Georgetown, D.C. (Library of Congress.)

11

So named because of the high topography of the land, the Highlands was built *c.* 1783, probably by either William Carroll or his father, Daniel Carroll III, son of Daniel Carroll of Rock Creek. The property bordered both the Carrolls' Rock Creek home and Edgewood plantation. Both the Highlands and Edgewood plantations raised tobacco and utilized the hilly topography to assist in rolling hogsheads of tobacco to Rock Creek to float to Georgetown for trade. In later years, according to Edith Ray Saul, her grandfather sold the tobacco at the Highlands but never smoked it, as the quality was too poor. The house was rebuilt as many as three times as it changed owners. Once a substantial and thriving farm, the fields gave way, as did many other lower Montgomery County farms, to poor soil conditions and suburban development. (Edith Ray Saul, courtesy Save Our Seminary.)

This bucolic scene greeted many visitors from before 1800 until the mid-1960s when the U.S. Army burned the old Maryland manse to make room for their commissary. Built by the Brent family, the Edgewood plantation house belonged to Robert Brent and Anne Carroll, whose son, Robert Young Brent, later became the first mayor of Washington, D.C. Just within the front door, a dining room was located to the right and a parlor to the left. The second floor contained two bedrooms, as did the attic space, which were likely servants' quarters. A road called Ireland Drive led away from the house to Rock Creek and is still in use today. (Authors' collection.)

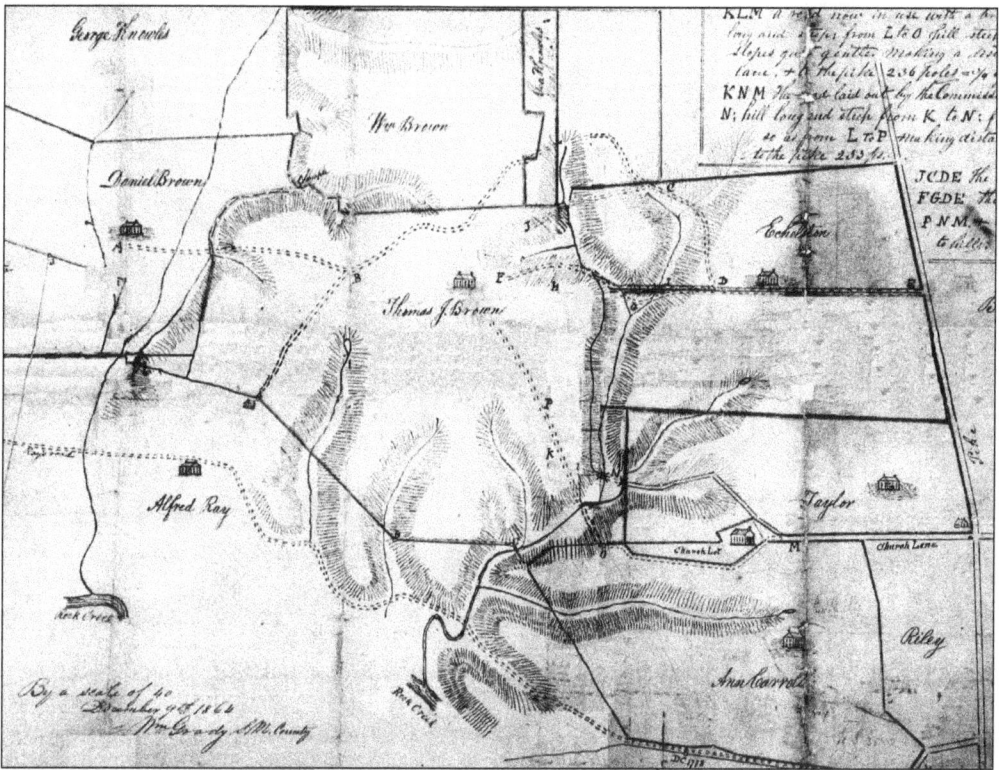

Off scale and primitive, this map is one of the earliest showing the area before arrival of the railroad. The dotted lines represent dirt streets, and the solid lines represent property boundaries or maintained roads. Ray's Road, which dots the property of Alfred Ray's Highlands Plantation, was previously known as Highland Road. Today, the easternmost portion is known as Linden Lane, and about where it crosses the creek, it becomes Newcastle Avenue. The road to the right is the old Brookeville and Washington Turnpike, today's Georgia Avenue. Church Lane is Forest Glen Road, and Ann Carroll's home is the old Carroll family home. Edgewood plantation is located just outside the image below the 1778 survey mark. (Authors' collection.)

Typical on tobacco farms, scenes like this were repeated daily at the Highlands and Edgewood plantations. Tobacco farming was hard work, and though it reaped great financial rewards, it depleted the soil faster than just about any other cash crop. Many farmers used their tobacco for trade as well. In this scene, slaves are cultivating, washing, and drying the leaves. The hogsheads were rolled down to Rock Creek and floated to the Port of Georgetown for sale or trade. (Library of Congress.)

Representing a terrible era in our history, slaves were found at many farms in lower Montgomery County. This engraving shows the arduous task of plowing a field before planting tobacco crops. Hundreds, sometimes thousands, of acres needed plowing. Another strenuous task was watering; the young girl in the image seems pensive at the well, perhaps contemplating the mindless chore and thinking of freedom. Many natural springs and creeks in this area made the water supply abundant, but ascending the hilly terrain to retrieve it was often exhausting. (Library of Congress.)

Edgewood plantation once contained over 300 acres. Though it began as a tobacco farm, the soil was quickly depleted of nutrients and it became a dairy and poultry farm. Six documented antebellum cabins sat on the farm in 1928 when it was purchased by the last private owner, James Eli Ament. In this photo, contemporary with Ament's purchase, several girls from National Park Seminary lounge about the old place, mindless of the turbulent past the previous occupants would have endured. The enormous hand-hewn and weathered logs give way to what had been an exterior fireplace, long closed in when this picture was taken. The porch is a recent addition. The cabin was demolished sometime between 1942 and 1951. (Authors' collection.)

14

The last antebellum cabin remained standing long after the army purchased the farm in 1942. Close inspection by the author prior to its dismantling in 1989 revealed hundreds of hand-cut pieces of local quartzite and schist, known as "chinking," which was used for fill between the logs. Obvious handmade cuts prevail on every log with the exception of the porch, which was likely added in the early 1900s. The first floor was a large, open room with a small kitchen and interior/exterior fireplaces. The second floor contained a loft. The family seated here worked for the last private owner of the property as tenant farmers and most likely lived in nearby Lyttonsville. The photo was titled "Uncle Tom's Cabin" when taken in 1928. This building was located in the vicinity of today's Army Post Exchange gas station. (Authors' collection.)

Better insulated for the cold, this clapboard structure (though likely a hewn-log cabin in disguise) was situated in an unknown location on Alfred Ray's Highland estate. However, the structure likely dates to the period when the Carrolls or Brents owned the farm, nearly 100 years prior to Ray's arrival. Local historian Edith Ray Saul says the center chimney structure was known as Henry Clay's cabin. Henry Clay did visit the Brent family here, but Clay's connection to this house is yet to be established. The Highlands had slaves, though this image dates after emancipation. The two girls are from the Highlands estate and likely from the Moore family. The African-American family were likely tenant farmers descended from Ray's slaves. (Edith Ray Saul collection.)

15

A walk in the nearby woods of the Edgewood plantation today yields many clues of the old farm, particularly tree growth. Many trees appear to be 60 to 80 years old, which is about the time the fields were abandoned for crops and adopted as pastures, as can be seen in this 1928 photo. The changes made after 1942 to the topography of this area are substantial. The ridge just above the grazing cows is the location of Stephen Sitter Avenue today. The barely visible structure on the far left is a rabbit and hen house, long demolished. Much of this land has been leveled out for creation of a baseball field and helicopter landing pad. (Authors' collection.)

Several barns were rebuilt upon original foundations dating prior to 1800, when Edgewood was built. Less the large structure in the foreground, they are located today along Stephen Sitter Avenue near the Walter Reed Army Institute of Research serving as storage and a physical fitness center. In this image dating to about 1929, the farm has essentially abandoned tobacco and other cultivating and focuses on raising chickens, pigs, and cows for local sale and private use. The property lines of the Edgewood plantation existed along Rock Creek to the vicinity of the beltway, to the railroad tracks, to Brookeville Road, and back to Rock Creek. (Authors' collection.)

16

Fodder, about to be offloaded into one of Edgewood's barns, as well as other minor crops, was raised strictly as animal feed in Forest Glen. Pictured here are two tenant farmers, likely residents in nearby Lyttonsville, who worked for James Eli Ament, the last private owner of the farm. The image dates to about 1929; the barns are second generation but believed to have been built upon original foundations. Today, the land behind the barn is a baseball field and helicopter landing pad, while the barns are used for storage and a gym. (Authors' collection.)

The Victorianized Highlands, holding the Ray clan on its front porch c. 1875, would soon change ownership before its demise after World War II. This house is believed to be the second built on the original foundation laid by Daniel Carroll III. Before its demise, the property had nearly 300 acres, much of which was purchased and subdivided for new home construction between the 1930s and late 1970s. Today known as Rock Creek Hills, the area was once part of the Carrolls' Rock Creek tract and later Forest Glen. Residential development before World War II and construction of the Capital Beltway in the 1960s forever divided the neighborhood. (Edith Ray Saul, courtesy Save Our Seminary.)

Nicolas Jones is seen c. 1900 on the porch of his ancestral home, Clean Drinking Manor, in lower Montgomery County. Located where Jones Bridge Road and Jones Mill Road intersect, the farm competed with Edgewood and Highlands, less than two miles away. Little social interaction seems to have taken place between the families; however, all three probably used the modest Jones' Mill, now gone. The Jones property consisted of a tract granted to John Coats in 1699. The manor, built shortly thereafter, stood until after World War II, when it collapsed onto itself. Rumors of workers from Mount Vernon salvaging bricks like those in the chimney have been lore since the author was a child; indeed, the two homes were near contemporaries. A spring grotto, believed to have spurred the name "Clean Drinking," is still located below the home site, now occupied by a nursing and rehabilitation center. (Authors' collection.)

The actual date that Rock Creek Chapel was erected is uncertain. Father Carroll arrived home to Rock Creek in 1773. Some believe the structure was built that year or the next; others believe it was built a few years earlier by his sister Ann. John Clagget Proctor wrote that the original church was built in 1774 and soon demolished for a larger one in 1777. Others believe it was built in 1783. Regardless, it is important to remember that this was the second Catholic church in the United States and the first under secular clergy. Its origins were poetically acknowledged by Rev. Thomas O'Gorman during the dedication of the third Saint John's, when he related, "If Baltimore is the Jerusalem—the Holy City of the Catholic Church, Rock Creek Chapel is its Bethlehem." This building stood for 82 years, was demolished, and then rebuilt in 1934 upon its original foundation by the Father Rosensteel Council, Knights of Columbus, Forest Glen. (Contemporary image, author's collection.)

18

The second Saint John's Church, constructed in 1850, replaced the small and dilapidated structure described above, the first building to be called "Saint John's." Of simple wood frame and siding, the second church lasted a mere 43 years until it needed to be replaced. Located between the current one and the previous one, it was demolished in 1893. (Saint John the Evangelist Church.)

The third Saint John's Church and Rectory was designed by famed Baltimore & Ohio (B&O) Railroad architect E.F. Baldwin, a devout Catholic and frequenter to Forest Glen. It competed for architectural fanfare with the train station, designed by his office six years earlier in 1887. Dedicated by Cardinal Gibbons, archbishop of Baltimore, the church, which still stands today, was built using beautiful Seneca Creek sandstone. Surrounding it are tombs bearing many notable names of people who shaped the nation and the community, including Young, Brent, and of course, Carroll. Memorial markers for both John and Daniel Carroll are found in the graveyard as well. (Authors' collection.)

Indian Rock, a local landmark for hundreds of years, was destroyed by the State for realignment of Jones Mill Road and construction of a bridge over Rock Creek c. 1967. In this c. 1910 view, girls from the neighboring National Park Seminary picnic next to the old familiar sight. Local legend states this to be a marker on an old Indian trail, several of which existed in the area. Others believe that the profile of a Native American at rest can be seen. The image was taken from the intersection of today's Forsythe Avenue and Jones Mill Road. A bike path today occupies the old road. (Authors' collection.)

This is the earliest known image of the bridge over Rock Creek behind the Edgewood farm. Possibly built by the Keys, Jones, or perhaps Brent families, the bridge is a primitive structure of logs spanning the creek. Known as Ireland Drive, the road led from the Edgewood plantation down to the creek, across it, and onto the neighboring Jones property; it also later served as part of Jones Mill Road. Today, the area remains wetlands inhabited by a vast array of animals, thanks in part to wildlife management and support efforts by the neighboring Audubon Society. The nearby "cliffs" of Forest Glen tell the fascinating story of how Rock Creek, for millions of years, has meandered its way towards the Potomac River. Most of the area is controlled and maintained by the Maryland National Capital Park and Planning Commission. (Authors' collection.)

Girls from National Park Seminary gather in this peaceful spot by the old mill stream about 1915. Little did they know, Jones' Mill, built before the Revolution, once stood directly across from them. Today, dozens of people transverse here between Rock Creek Park and Forest Glen. The truss bridge, which was the third bridge here, was dismantled and disposed of in the creek; at times of low water, it can be seen just below the new bridge, the fifth on the site. The woods around the girls was for many years pasture belonging to the Edgewood plantation and, hundreds of years before, was said to have been the site of an old Indian road. Evidence of Native American presence has recently been discovered and abounds on the bluffs above Rock Creek. (Authors' collection.)

Alfred Ray's Quarry, located along the Metropolitan Branch of the B&O Railroad between Forest Glen and Kensington, became a favorite swimming hole when it was abandoned after about 1920. Most construction in the area prior to 1920 utilized stone from here. Ray's farm failed because of poor soil conditions, but he remained successful in the quarry business, especially when the railroad arrived. In this c. 1955 photo, the Kensington Volunteer Fire Department prepares to remove a shivering young man who fell through the ice and became trapped on a small islet. Ray's quarry was filled in after several others drowned. New homes were later developed along Pratt Street atop the quarry in what is today Capitol View. Note the railroad tracks at left. (Kensington Volunteer Fire Department.)

21

Two feet into the earth, hand-cut, and out of its natural element, this massive piece of quartzite sits where Ireland Drive and the road to the old Jones' Mill meet in the woods below the old Edgewood plantation. It is more than likely a boundary stone, as such use of rocks and trees is prevalent in early maps showing property lines. Early records do not clarify if the Carrolls, Brents, or Joneses held rights to Rock Creek; it was likely the latter. This could also mark the flood plain or high water line of Rock Creek, preventing the farmer from seeding land and risking it washing away. It could also be a road marker of significant age, as many believe these now paved "bike paths" originated as Indian trails. (Contemporary photo, authors' collection.)

Found on the old Edgewood farm, this stone may mark the grave of a slave or tenant farmer from as far back as the early 1700s, or perhaps an early settler or explorer. Or perhaps it is the grave of a Confederate soldier, wounded at the battle of Fort Stevens, who died here in retreat; 17 other Confederates killed in the raid are buried about a mile from this spot. It is also possible this is the grave of McFonso, one of the Keys' prized racehorses, who, after a successful career at local tracks, died at the age of 24 and was buried on the farm about 1917. The stone bears no discernable inscription and is located about 100 yards off Ireland Drive near Woodstock Court and the site of a recently identified, small mill. The stone, about four feet long, is hand-chiseled in a somewhat crude manner and is buried at least three feet into the earth. (Contemporary photo, authors' collection.)

22

Lookout House, so aptly named, stood for many years above the cliffs of Rock Creek near Indian Rock on today's Wilton Avenue. It was built by a real-estate conglomerate that came to the area to develop new homes in 1887. This image gives a good example of the steep and rocky cliffs that create the southwest edge of the neighborhood above Rock Creek Park. Many believe Alfred Ray quarried this area as well. (Authors' collection.)

A serene view from Covington Lane looks across fields belonging to Clean Drinking Manor. The small structure on the lower right is Lookout House. The view is towards Bethesda, and the same view today yields high-rises, the Capital Beltway, and the National Naval Medical Center. The area was appealing to settlers as early as the late 1600s because of its abundance of fowl, fish, and game, as well as nutrient-rich soil, good drainage, and many springs and streams. The close proximity to Washington would later become an asset and a harbinger of change in the form of development, as the sun was setting on lower Montgomery County farms. (Montgomery County Historical Society.)

Two

Cum Natura Non Contra

With Nature, Not Against

The Carroll home became the Carroll Springs Sanitarium *c.* 1887. Locally known as the "San," it was owned by Dr. George Wright, who promised a quiet, healing environment with medicinal baths from seven springs. Nearby railroads had made Forest Glen a tourist stop and a renowned healing spa catering to Washington elite. Additions to the Carroll home accommodated patients and those in need of a few days' respite. Wright's wife was the second woman to graduate from the University of Chicago; their daughter Lucy Wright Trundle became the first woman on the Montgomery County Board of Education and was active in community affairs, while Katherine Wright, M.D., owned and managed the San until its demolition shortly after World War II, was a renowned leader in women's health, and became a doctor at an early age. (Save Our Seminary.)

Carroll Springs Sanitarium
WASHINGTON, D. C.

IN THE SUBURBS.

OPEN ALL THE YEAR.

A Rest Resort in Summer; A Health Home in Winter. Combines all the advantages of the country with those of the city; all the benefits of a home life with those to be derived from an institution. **Pure Spring Water** piped through the buildings.

Baths, Electricity, Sun Parlor, Covered Verandas, Hot Water Heat, Open Fires, Acetylene Gas. Fresh Fruits and Vegetables, Eggs and Milk from the Sanitarium Farm.

Brightwood Electric Cars within two minutes walk. B. & O. R. R. Station near.

SEND FOR ILLUSTRATED BOOKLET.

ADDRESS

G. H. WRIGHT, M. D., FOREST GLEN, MARYLAND.

LONG DISTANCE TELEPHONE, 117-3-TAKOMA.

25

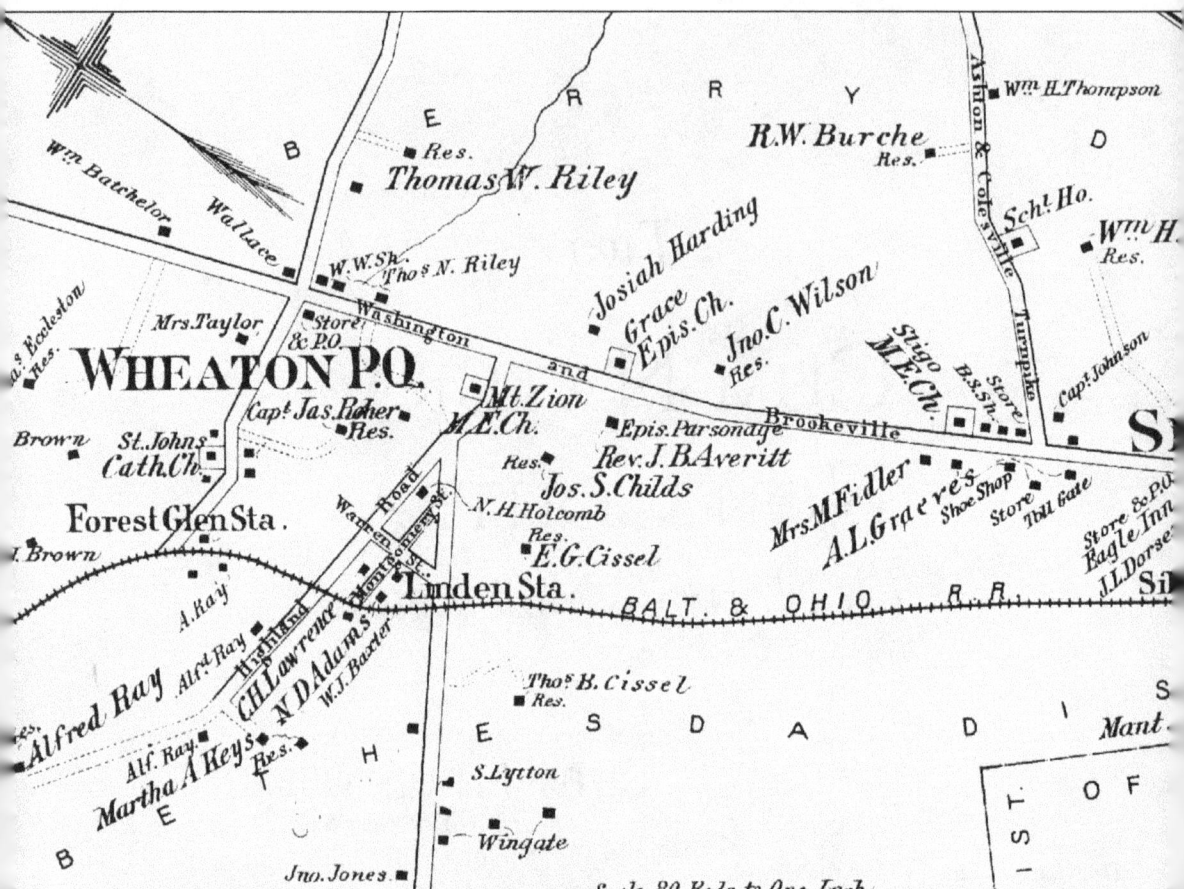

In 1873, the Metropolitan Branch of the B&O Railroad arrived in Montgomery County, serving the Edgewood farm via Linden Station (now demolished), located about 50 yards south of the Linden Lane crossing, and the Highlands farm via the Forest Glen Station. Some farmers sold their land for new residential development; the Keys family developed Linden, an early suburban community, at the intersection of Montgomery Street and Warren Street off Highland Road (now Linden Lane). Close inspection of this map, created in 1878 but updated to show the railroad in 1893, yields such important local names as Ray, Keys, Lytton, Jones, Eccleston, and Childs. The latter owned a substantial farm located in today's Montgomery Hills around the water tower. The road coming from the bottom of the image is the old Brookeville and Tenallytown Road. (Save Our Seminary.)

Built in 1887, Forest Glen Railroad Station was designed by the office of Edwin Frances Baldwin, the noted architect who created or oversaw designs for most of the region's B&O stations and outbuildings. A devout Catholic, he often visited Forest Glen, the location of another of his works, the third Saint John's Forest Glen church. This is one of the earliest images of Forest Glen station known to exist. The signal tower in the front is a telltale sign that the image was taken before 1908, when all block signals were automated. In later years, a tunnel kept pedestrians from crossing the tracks, and a waiting shelter was built across from the station. The map at right, from the Germantown Historical Society, relates the density of stations and bedroom communities in Montgomery County, Maryland, by 1893.

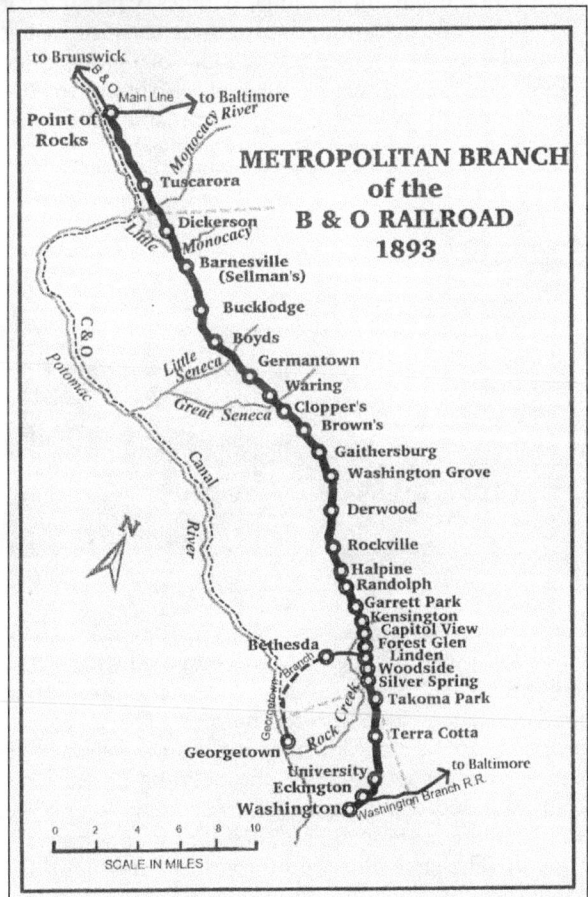

Ye Forest Inne, as drawn by Thomas Franklin Schneider, was built in the Queen Anne style with a wide encircling veranda, porches, bays, and varied towers. The foundation used local quartzite, while trees from the site were used in the framing. The entire structure was covered in wood shingles. The inn was the idea of a group of local businessmen naming themselves the Forest Glen Improvement Company, who hoped to prosper from selling land for new homes and appealing to the resort crowd. They renamed the 88 acres they purchased from the Highlands farm "Forest Glen Park." (Authors' collection.)

Completed in 1887, the building competed with other resorts cum–real estate ventures in the Washington suburbs, including Glen Echo and Bethesda. Chevy Chase Land Company had similar interests as well. None but the latter prospered and still survives today. In the center pediment above the front steps is a beautiful stained-glass window with Ye Forest Inne spelled out. A summer retreat only, the building closed for the winter. Within two years, a boiler plant was added and year-round accommodations were offered. Shortly thereafter, alcohol and gambling were instituted, despite protests from Fr. Charles O. Rosensteel at Saint John's Church. The large observation tower offered views as far as Washington, D.C., and Sugarloaf Mountain. (Authors' collection.)

The main entrance hall (above) greeted every guest. Typical of the period was the fretwork and stained glass. Guest registration was to the right and the dining hall to the left. The 47 guest rooms booked for about $2 a night. At the end of each hall were found the water closets, and rooms closer to them were subject to an additional 50¢. The second-floor parlor (below), directly above the one on the first floor, was referred to as the ladies' parlor. Though fireplaces are original to the building's construction, they were not used until 1890 when the building was opened year-round. The inn was managed by Tenney & Company, proprietors of National Hotel in Washington, D.C. (Authors' collection.)

The inn's architect, Thomas Franklin Schneider, though never formally schooled in architecture, was one of Washington's masters. He studied as an apprentice under renowned architect Adolph Cluss with the firm of Cluss and Shultz and later opened an office on F Street Northwest in Washington, D.C. His many works include hundreds of D.C. row houses and the Cairo Hotel, Washington's first steel skyscraper and inspiration for the city's building height restriction. Schneider married Mary Osbourne Beach in 1891, and after a successful career that included Thomas Franklin Schneider Jr. and Harry Wardman as protégés, he retired in 1923. (Historical Society of Washington.)

Ye Forest Inne's dining hall, one of the region's first, and kitchens were designed to feed well over 100 people, which was well in excess of the 47-room capacity. Old Maryland favorites, including seafood, were available on the daily menu thanks to railroad deliveries. In the evenings, the dining hall was cleared and band concerts, if not outside, were given, as well as weekend dances. (Authors' collection.)

The footbridge lessened the arduous task of crossing the glen and stream between the inn and station. Made of decorative cast iron with wood planking and log abutments, the structure was built in 1887 by the Berlin Iron Bridge Company of East Berlin, Connecticut, for $3,000. The span was about 100 feet long by 60 feet wide and descended slightly from the inn side. Visitors to the inn could cross the bridge, but baggage-men and carriages had to follow the road below. (Authors' collection.)

A copy of an old English rectory, this home, later named Braemar, was built by the Forest Glen Improvement Company as an example of the palatial homes envisioned for the neighborhood. The inn also used the building as a gathering place for ladies. Meanwhile, the men were escorted by the improvement company developers into the woods to search the land for the ideal lot on which to build a new home. Unfortunately, not much was usually accomplished, and by 1892, only a handful of homes had been built.

Adding to the inn's appeal, a putting green was developed for the guests. Though short lived, the putting greens were popular, as were horseback riding, tennis, croquet, archery, bowling, and various other games. Many gave way to gambling, instituted when the owners realized real estate was not paying the bills. A national financial crisis, real estate crash, and considerable improvements in Washington, D.C., thwarted people's desires to move to the suburbs. Declining into bankruptcy, FGIC closed the inn at the end of the 1892 season. (Authors' collection.)

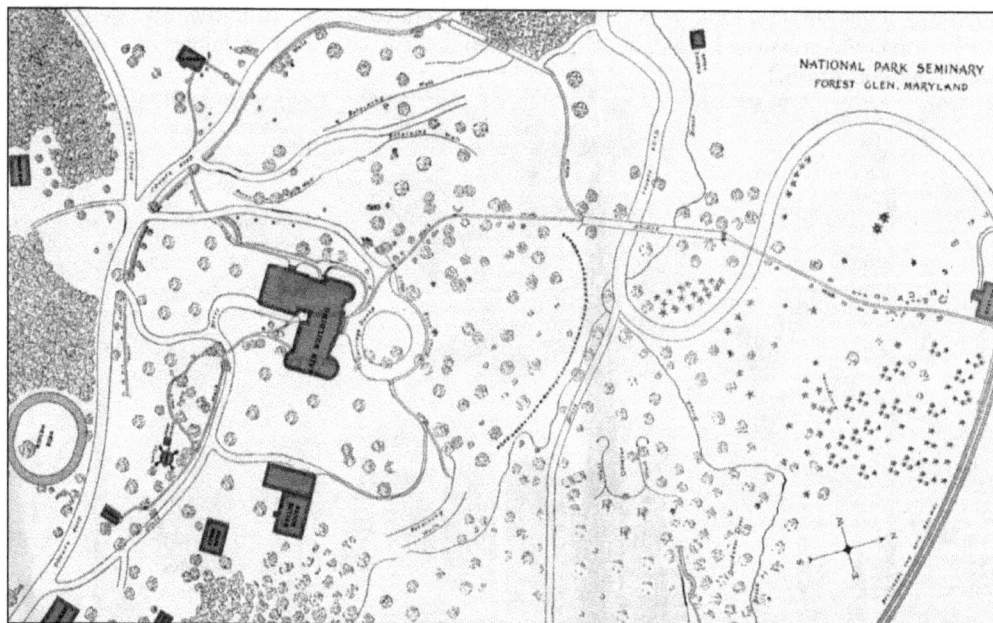

Forest Glen Park in 1894 was just a handful of homes (outside the map), a few outbuildings, the inn, the steam plant, and a few pump-houses. In 1893, John and Vesta Cassedy, educators from Norfolk, Virginia, met Thomas Franklin Schneider, whose new wife, Mary, had previously studied under them. The Cassedys were traveling the East Coast looking at potential sites to develop a girls' finishing school. Schneider directed them to Forest Glen, and despite visiting Woodlawn in Rockville and other similar failed hotels, the Cassedys chose Ye Forest Inne, with its woods, close proximity to the city, rail line, and space for expansion. (Author's Collection.)

John A.I. Cassedy and Vesta Harvey
Cassedy were students at Ohio Wesleyan
when they met. After graduation,
John taught at Lasell Seminary in
Massachusetts, while Vesta taught at
the Central College in Missouri. Later,
they married, taught, and presided over
the Young Women's College in Norfolk,
Virginia. There they decided to open
a school of higher education for girls,
known as a seminary. Their choice of
Ye Forest Inne and adjoining property,
which bordered the nationally owned
Rock Creek Park, led them to name the
school National Park Seminary (NPS).
The seminary's motto was Cum Natura
Non Contra, meaning With Nature,
Not Against. (Save Our Seminary.)

Ye Forest Inne was immediately renamed Main, and a massive rush to open the school in
September 1894 began. Nearly $5,000 was spent to remodel gambling halls into classrooms.
The Cassedys, who initially leased the property, purchased it in 1897, but only about half of the
original acreage was included. The remainder was used for new home sites. The first class was
comprised of 48 female students. This image, contemporary with the Cassedys' reign, was taken
after 1900 when an addition to the dining room was built and a glass-covered walkway added to
keep girls from inclement weather. (Authors' collection.)

The Cassedys implemented a 10-year building program during the first school year. They built a small home for themselves, which after just five years was expanded into a dormitory for freshmen. In later years, it included juniors. The image above is one of the earliest known of the house, known as Aloha, which today is overwhelmed by years of additions. It was constructed in 1898. (Save Our Seminary.)

National Park Seminary was Christian but non-sectarian. The first few years, no chapel was on the site, so a small part of the dining room was cleared for this function, as seen here. The parlor chairs are left over from the inn, as the Cassedys purchased an enormous collection of Chippendale chairs for their dining room. The room was also rearranged at times to serve as a social hall. (Authors' collection.)

The gymnasium was found in the gabled front of Main and was only used until 1907, when a new gymnasium was built behind there. Students had strict physical fitness requirements, and a good portion of their day was spent in this room or about the grounds, partaking in running, bicycling, archery, golfing, horse-back riding, walking, and softball. After the new gymnasium was built, this room was demolished for an addition to the dining room. (Authors' collection.)

John Cassedy also founded the Washington, Woodside and Forest Glen trolley, a line chartered from Washington to Forest Glen via Georgia Avenue, up Seminary Road, and to its terminus near Post Office Road. Seen here is one of the few Washington Woodside and Forest Glen cars; note the misspelling. With the trolley came overhead power lines; Cassedy routed a feeder line from Brightwood, D.C., to Forest Glen and used the voltage to turn roto-converters, or dynamos, at NPS, converting the power into 110 volts DC. By 1910, the entire campus was electrified. The trolley line was used until interrupted by construction of an underpass at the B&O crossing in Silver Spring. The Forest Glen trolley was replaced by bus service in 1925. (Pennsylvania Historical Society.)

In 1898, the Cassedys constructed a chapel just behind Main and had to enlarge it twice to meet increasing enrollment. Students were allowed to travel locally for denominational services. The chapel was also used as a meeting place before embarking on trips to Washington. Stained-glass windows seen in the chapel today were a gift from the first graduating class. (Authors' collection.)

When a new student entered National Park Seminary for the first time, she was led by an upperclasswoman through the heavy double doors of Main to here, the main entrance parlor. The impression left on freshmen entering Main for the first time was unique and just the beginning of special events and places the student would experience year-round. Everything a National Park Seminary girl needed to understand about her pampered school life began here. (Authors' collection.)

After entering the main entrance parlor, a student who walked down the hall and looked to the right would see this view. Persian rugs randomly scattered about the floor were a novel idea and typically Victorian despite the beautiful hardwood floors beneath. Much of the furniture and décor were remnants of the failed hotel and were sold with the buildings. Note the stick and ball fretwork in the main reception parlor behind the fireplace. (Authors' collection.)

Main reception parlor, also known as the empire parlor, was located behind the large fireplace in the main entrance parlor. This room became a welcoming haven for visitors and new students alike. The Victorianism is almost overwhelming but typical of the well-to-do. In all, seven parlors of different themes were found throughout Main. (Authors' collection.)

Main dining room, which reputedly had the largest collection of Chippendale chairs known to exist, was to the left of the main entrance parlor. Within 20 years, the dining room was enlarged to seat 400. Dinner was a formal affair, and special clothes or "evening wear" were a must-have for every student. Girls celebrating birthdays or special events could have cake and private parties; girls feeling under the weather or too overwhelmed to make it to dinner could have their meals delivered to their rooms. The painting is by Santerre and titled "The Girl and the Candle." (Authors' collection.)

The Forest Glen Trading Company, built by George Wolfe around 1900, served as an apartment on the second floor and the Miller and Wolfe store on the first. Wolfe later worked for the Cassedys, and his daughter later attended NPS. A local resident named Fowler built and opened what is today the Forest Glen Country store, seen here on the far right. The trading company burned down shortly after this image was taken, was rebuilt, and was given the castle-like roof seen today by the second owner of NPS, James Eli Ament. Between these two buildings at one time was a the Engle family's home, which was moved c. 1911 to its present site at the rear of the trading company. The Engle boys rode the whole trip on the porch! (Authors' collection.)

Sororities were accidentally introduced to the school by Mary Charlotte Priest, an English teacher who corralled a select group of literary honor students and held meetings in an area just off the old gym. When it was discovered, the Cassedys decided to allow the entire student body to form sororities and later insisted that every student be a member of one. This American bungalow, constructed in 1896, was the first sorority house built, for the second sorority formed, Alpha Epsilon Pi. The houses were merely for meetings and were constructed on a garden scale without kitchens or bathrooms. Such domestic additions would not come until two decades later. (Authors' collection.)

NPS's first sorority received the second house. Chi Omicron Pi, or Chiopi, was the first organized. Built in 1899 in the Ho-O-Den or Phoenix style, the Japanese bungalow was the first of what became an architecturally eclectic campus. The Cassedys had with them in 1894 a booklet on international styles, a souvenir of their visit to the World's Columbia Exposition in Chicago. From this book came many of the sorority construction plans. Behind Chiopi to the right is Glencoe House, a private dwelling built on land belonging to the Forest Glen Improvement Company. (Authors' collection.)

Chapter House, also known as Mother Sorority House, was built before 1900 for sororities that had organized but did not have a meeting house. After 1906, when all eight sorority houses had been built on the campus—four on the east side and four on the west, the structure was moved across Linden Lane and became Recitation Hall, as student enrollment required more classroom space. The groups of girls leaving the building are probably coming from sorority meetings. The structure to the left is the gym. (Authors' collection.)

Senior House was a dormitory for the senior class. In this image, shortly after the house's construction, Hebe, the Greek goddess of youth, offers her salutation on a crisp fall morning in 1899. The Cassedys placed special emphasis on the seniors to lead the school and set proper examples for the younger students. Furthermore, seniors were about to embark into the world where they represented NPS. Each senior also had the duty of turning a new student into her protégé; this was done through the sororities, and the two would interact the entire year. (Authors' collection.)

Probably the most important building constructed by the school, the Odeon, which is Greek for theater, was built in 1901 and was the first to be electrified. The seating and balconies sat nearly the entire student body, and there was a large orchestra pit and large fly-stage. Designed for its acoustics, it was also used for recital and baccalaureate services. The building's quiet setting was admired equally inside and out. The structure housing the fly-stage is seen to the left of the eyebrow windows. (Authors' collection.)

Heavily indulged in by NPS girls, the arts, particularly dramatics, music, and dancing, were subjects some later pursued as careers. Most notable was Irene Castle. In this image, c. 1902, a recital is given by the lower class, led by NPS's musical director, Almon W. Vincent. This image relates about one-quarter of the Odeon's seating capacity. To the left of the piano is the orchestra pit, empty for tonight's recital. (Authors' collection.)

The Cassedys' most expensive improvement to the campus, the new gymnasium, seen after its construction in 1907, had a double-branched stairway divided by a ticket booth. The second floor had a large court for basketball, dance, and calisthenics. The lower level contained a double bowling alley, a heated swimming pool, and locker room, with the novel idea "needle baths," or showers. The rear of the building, at right, contained a solarium, where a girl could take a vital sunbath. The unknown building to the far right may have been moved to serve as a servant's cottage. A massive front portico with enormous columns completed the building as a Greek temple after the Recitation House was moved from the front. A one-story building with a bowling alley built for the inn was demolished for the gym's construction. (Authors' collection.)

Whimsical spots such as this at NPS were as common as concrete in today's world. This gazebo, overlooking the athletic fields on the south side of Linden Lane, was built on tree stumps along Linden Lane. NPS had its own carpenters and groundskeepers who lived on the site, working year-round repairing and maintaining the buildings and creating fun places like this. The fence ran around much of the athletic fields, which if in existence today would border Linden Lane, Stephen Sitter Avenue, and Ireland Drive.

North of the athletic fields were the tennis courts, which survived after being installed for patrons of the inn. These appear to be clay courts, and more than likely the games were staged for the camera, as the girls are playing in their school uniforms. The road in the background is Linden Lane, the building is the stable, and the small cottage in the rear is the carpenter's cottage. (Authors' collection.)

Equestrians stand on Linden Lane on a mild winter's day in 1912. Horseback riding was a necessity and an enjoyable sport before automobiles, and nearly every NPS girl rode. Many weekly competitions were judged by army officers from nearby Walter Reed Army Hospital. To the rear are the new stables, as the first burned down in 1910. The stables were built well away from Main with the formal rose garden between the two. Girls could bring their own horses and board them at the stables or ride the school's horses. A tack room was located on the lower level of the gabled tower. The massive eagle was a standard in the Washington area; this bird was destroyed by vandals in 1983, but two similar examples are found at the entrance gates to the Soldier's Home, a retirement home for soldiers and airmen, in Washington, D.C., today. (Authors' collection.)

Built in 1907, the Italian Villa was one of five dormitories at NPS. Adding another chapter of international style, it was a favorite among students and one of only a handful of this Italian design in the Washington region. This image, taken from the Drive Bridge, shows a small portion of the formal gardens that make up a true Italian villa. Each twin tower contained dorm rooms, and every school year, a drawing was held to find the lucky occupants. The road in the foreground extended through the glen to Rock Creek Park. (Authors' collection.)

Gardens were the pillar of the campus, and each building complemented, or was complemented by, numerous gardens, statuary, and stone work. The gardens were for the most part formal, and the seminary employed 50 gardeners to maintain the grounds daily. Perhaps the most aesthetic was the glen itself. In fall of 1910, this group of girls are on the steps leading up to justice court, where a colossal statue of blind justice stands watch above the glen. The formal gardens program was begun by the Cassedys in 1896. (Authors' collection.)

The house for Zeta Eta Theta, built in 1899, was designed by founders of the sorority as a Swiss chalet. It was the largest and on a more domestic scale than the others. Here, the house stands on the road leading from the circle of Main. Two decades later, Zeta was moved to its present location on Linden Lane to make room for construction of the ballroom. NPS used different foundation stone at different times—including quartzite, schist, and blue quartzite—which often suggest the age of the buildings. (Authors' collection.)

One of the most whimsical buildings on the campus is Kappa Delta Phi's Dutch windmill. Built in 1899 from plans in the Cassedys' architectural book, the structure was most likely a lighthouse or seaside cottage–cum windmill because of its location. Stationary windmill arms were positioned on the widow's walk using a large hook. In the background is the Drive Bridge. (Authors' collection.)

Phi Delta Psi, built in 1903, was originally intended to be a Roman triumphal arch, or gatehouse, but topography of the land and the lot size dedicated to the neighboring Kappa windmill prevented such. Instead, the building was constructed as an early American Colonial home, and the Doric columns intended for the Roman triumphal arch were later used in construction of the Practice House nearby. The large archway was intended for the road in the foreground; instead, the arch was closed in and became a parlor. This design also came from the Cassedys' book of plans. The structure behind Delta is the Pergola Bridge. In later years, both end porches were covered and the rear enclosed. (Authors' collection.)

Peeping Tom, as this statue of Hiawatha was nicknamed, stands peering through the large, parlor window of Theta Sigma Rho, a Spanish mission built for the sorority in 1903. Filled with artifacts from the arts and crafts period, the sorority was located on the westernmost boundary. The roof offered a wonderful garden patio used year-round. This structure also came from the Cassedys' book of plans. Later named Edgewood II, the house in the background was owned by NPS and is a Sears catalog home. (Authors' collection.)

46

Perhaps the most recognized and admired building in Montgomery County, the Japanese pagoda of Chi Psi Upsilon sorority was built in 1905. Though many believe this style is more Chinese, the building completed the architectural folly that is Forest Glen Park. Unfortunately, not everyone was pleased with its construction, particularly Chiopi—the Japanese bungalow. So many arguments arose between the two sororities over who had the more authentic Japanese home that Mrs. Cassedy remodeled the latter, with approval of the girls, into an American bungalow. The Japanese lanterns are reputedly 400 years old. (Authors' collection.)

Perfectly situated at the head of the glen, this English garden castle was built in 1904 for Pi Beta Nu as the final sorority house to be constructed. The bridge in the foreground is a pseudo drawbridge, complete with chains and pulleys, fixed to the castle. Beta girls were given the title of gatekeepers to the NPS property, as their castle was the first structure encountered when entering the campus. The castle had a roof garden offering scenic views. Like other sorority houses, by 1920, this structure was enlarged and given a bathroom and kitchenette. (Authors' collection.)

47

Jahu Dewitt Miller, a noted orator who traveled the Chautauqua circuit, also collected important books. His collection exceeded 20,000, and he kept most volumes in a rail car while traveling or in storage in New York. The Cassedys befriended Miller in Norfolk and later invited him to stay at NPS when he spoke at Glen Echo. This evolved into a monthly visit, and in 1900, Dr. Cassedy suggested that Miller store his books in a library on NPS grounds and allow students their access. Miller agreed, and a building to house his collection was erected. Miller regularly gave speeches and the NPS commencement address until his death in 1911. (Authors' collection.)

In 1901, the Miller Library was constructed as the last shingle-style structure. It was located at the corner of Linden Lane and Forsythe Avenue, on the west side of campus, again using the book of plans from the Columbian Exposition for its design. The exterior stucco band relates the interior mezzanine level, an open space offering plenty of light. A porch overlooks NPS, and a fireplace made for cozy reading in winter months. In front of the building is a plaque memorializing Miller with the planting of trees in front of the library. NPS also had a library in the west wing of Main for studies. (Authors' collection.)

The Drive Bridge, or Castle Bridge, led from the foot of Kappa, across the first leg of the bifurcated glen, along a roadway in front of the Villa, across the deep ravine and Spring Branch, and then to an abutment below the train station. In later years, NPS owned a 12-cylinder Cadillac that shuttled students or other visiting dignitaries between the station and Main. The front entrance of NPS was accessed by this bridge, which today has been lost to the Capital Beltway. (Authors' collection.)

Pictured is Walk Bridge, or Honeysuckle Bridge, looking towards the train station in 1915. The tiny boxwoods in the circle have matured to over six feet tall today, and in the summertime, when the sun warms the oils in their leaves, the pithy perfume is a bittersweet reminder of all that's been lost at NPS. (Authors' collection.)

A favorite spot of every NPS girl, the spring grotto was one of the treasures built by Francisco Ginechesi. The arch exposes a year-round icy, crystal-clear spring that emerges and joins the glen. The stone walks and bridges spanned most of the glen from the Villa to the Sphinx Bridge. Today, this special nook is as vital and beautiful as ever, and it appeals to hundreds of visitors. Stalactites form inside the pointed arch, and the water is very deep.

The boat swings were located on the athletic field parallel to Linden Lane. On a warm fall day in 1915, NPS girls take turns pulling the overhead rope on the downswing; then the opposing girl does the same on the upswing thus causing the teeter-totter motion. (Authors' collection.)

The Haven was built for William D. Little on the old Forest Glen Improvement Company property in 1908, probably by Francisco Ginechesi. It was a private residence for a short time and then appeared in school catalogs as a residence for foreign language and poetry teachers. The walls are 20-inch granite blocks and were built around existing trees. The oak in the image still exists, but because of its present size, the present owners must notch the fascia board and roof. (Authors' collection.)

As viewed from Beta's drawbridge, a troupe of NPS girls area ready for a ride towards the Forest Glen train station sometime after 1915. Notice the rear addition to Kappa, which, along with the other seven sororities, was modernized with kitchenettes and bathrooms. (Authors' collection.)

National Park Seminary for Young Women					
AN AVERAGE STUDENT'S DAILY SCHEDULE					
Period	Tuesday	Wednesday	Thursday	Friday	Saturday
8.30 to 9.10	Recite Sociology	Recite Sociology	Recite Sociology	Study History	Recite Sociology
9.10 to 9.50	Study English	Study Sociology	Piano Practice	Piano Practice	Piano Practice
9.50 to 10.30	Recite English	Study History	Recite English	Recite English	Recite English
10.30 to 11.10	Cooking	Piano Practice	Study History	Gymnasium	Study English
11.10 to 11.50	Cooking	Music Lesson 40 m.	Study History	Music Lesson 20 m.	Study History
11.50 to 1.10	Chapel and Luncheon	Chapel and Luncheon	Chapel and Luncheon	Chapel and Luncheon	Chapel and Luncheon
1.10 to 1 50	Piano Practice	Study History	Piano Practice	Study History	Piano Practice
1.50 to 2.30	Piano Practice	Recite History	Recite History	Recite History	Recite History
2.30 to 4.10	Walk and Recreation	Walk and Recreation	Walk and Recreation	Walk and Recreation	2.30to 3.30 Recreation
4.10 to 4.50	Gymnasium	Study Sociology	Gymnasium	Study Sociology	3.30 Chorus
4.50 to 5.30	Gymnasium	Study English	Gymnasium	Study Sociology	4.00 Chorus
5.30 to 7.30	Dinner and Recreation	Dinner and Recreation	Dinner and Recreation	Dinner and Recreation	4.30 Study Sociology
7.30 to 8.10	Lecture	Study English	Lecture	Study English	5.00 Study Sociology
8.10 to 8.50	Study Sociology	Chorus	Study English	Study English	5.30 to 10.00 Recreation Dinner Free Evening
8.50 to 9.30	Study Sociology	Club Meeting	Study History	Study History	

The NPS school week was Tuesday through Saturday, with Sunday reserved for prayer and studies and Mondays including play and shopping in Washington. The local boys' school was out on Saturday, which accounted for this organization. For trips to Washington, NPS chartered a two-car train. Girls who did not go to Washington often went hiking or horseback riding, sometimes to the "house of the old hermit," where Nick Jones, shown in the previous chapter, lived. (Authors' collection.)

A massive stone stairway connected Honeysuckle Bridge to the Greek grotto, where plays and recitals in the open theater were given. Master stonework such as this was prevalent throughout the glen, though much of it is in ruins today. Walks, bridges, a springhouse, retaining walls, wells, and winding stairs were found throughout. In the summer months, this area of the glen stays about 10 to 15 degrees cooler than the rest and has been a favorite respite since the days of the inn. (Authors' collection.)

Ye Blue Bird, a soda fountain, was a tradition at NPS, offering ice cream, sodas, and social hour on a limited basis. The soda fountain, back bar (which appears to be a turn-of-the-century Brunswick, Balke, Collender & Co. model), and high booth seating may be remnants of the inn or items purchased by the Cassedys at auctions. The room and fountain was reconfigured to suit popular styles through the years. Here, we see NPS girls during an afternoon break in the winter of 1920. (Authors' collection.)

Clarence Bloomfield Moore, pictured atop Masterpiece, purchased the Highlands and about 300 acres bordering NPS *c.* 1900. A wealthy broker, Moore and his wife, Mabelle Swift Moore, owned real estate throughout the region. Two girls attending NPS named Swift and Moore were likely family members, and the latter claimed her home address as "Forsythe," probably what Mr. Moore renamed Highlands. Later known as Rock Creek Farms, it raised horses, cattle, and hounds. Today, Forsythe Avenue runs near the property lines of the old farm, which has been dissected from the neighborhood by the Capital Beltway. (Chevy Chase Club.)

As master of the fox hunt, Clarence Moore displays his world-renowned ability of controlling his hounds while hacking to a meet in 1906. The Moores also owned an affluent home at 1746 Massachusetts Avenue in D.C. and one in Loudoun, Virginia, where Moore began a foxhunt club. In 1912, he traveled to England to purchase 50 hounds, and on the return trip, he boarded the *Titanic*. The dogs returned safely on another vessel, but Moore and his servant Charles Harrington perished. The Highlands fell into neglect, and because Moore had left in his will that the land shouldn't be sold until his two children were of age, the land was not sold until 1929. The Continental Life Insurance Company bought the 300 acres and developed the well-planned bedroom community of Rock Creek Hills. (Chevy Chase Club.)

Trotting down Saul Road in 1907, whips George Curran and Shirley Sudduth follow huntsman Robert M. Curran with what appears to be the old Highlands in the background. Clarence Moore's "Chevy Chase Pack" scamper down the dirt road towards Kensington Parkway. Moore debated for many years bringing the fox hunt to this farm. With development and his tragic death, it never happened. The red fox species prevalent in the Rock Creek region were mostly introduced for the hunt and, as they have few predators other than man, have grown to a substantial population today. (Chevy Chase Club.)

54

Southeast of NPS was the Childs Farm, seen here ridding its apple orchards for new development as many of its counterparts did. The water tower on the site was first generation. This image was taken from the vicinity of 9302 Sutton Place, author Ric Nelson's childhood home. The same view today yields a county parking lot, Sniders, and Silver Spring Fire Station 19, where both authors spent much time in service to the community. (Suburban Trust Company of Silver Spring.)

Pictured is the west end of the campus from Zeta's porch in 1915. By the next decade, Zeta was moved from here to its current location to accommodate construction of a ballroom. From the left are the Chapel, Theta, Chiopi, Miller Library, ChiPsiU, and Glencoe House. By all means, NPS was entering into its golden age. The campus was nearly completed, and enrollment was annually beyond capacity. Waiting lists were common, and NPS administrators chose only those with the best references. NPS was also one of the most expensive finishing schools in the United States, catering to the world's financial elite. Student names such as Chrysler, Kraft, Swift, Hershey, Heinz, Spreckles, Wrigley, and Cromwell were commonplace. (Authors' collection.)

Built for senior class women, Senior House was later neighbored with Senior Annex, which accommodated increasing class numbers. Many senior classes planted ivy, which represents eternity, in front; the ivy came from such places as Stratford-on-Avon, Abbottsford, Newstead Abby, Gettysburg, Annapolis, Mount Vernon, and the homes of Edmond Rostand and Mark Twain. Marble plaques with class dates were set in the front of the building as well. Today, little evidence of the ivy remains, and the structures are in disrepair. The architectural detail of the porched addition is noteworthy, particularly the shingled wave pattern found in the twin gables and the hooded window between. The boxwoods in the foreground are today more than six feet tall and seen from the opposite angle on page 49. (Authors' collection.)

NPS uniforms were sailor suits, or middy blouses, custom made by Peter Thompson of New York. The dress uniform program was instituted by Mrs. Cassedy because in the early years, girls tried to out-dress each other. Guidelines were developed for what to wear during class, at leisure, on trips to Washington (which always included white gloves), at formal affairs, and at dinner. In front of the Senior House and the seated statue of Joan of Arc, these girls in 1916 wear school uniforms with the NPS logo stitched on the sleeve. Mrs. Cassedy passed away on Valentine's Day 1910, not seeing the positive impact her school dress program later had on the students. Dr. Cassedy lost much of his inspiration after Vesta's death and sold the entire campus by 1916. (Authors' collection.)

Interested in architecture and education, James Eli Ament purchased NPS, plus 40 acres and 3 lots, for $350,000 in September 1916. The only stipulation was that he follow the established curriculum, and Dr. Cassedy became an NPS board member to ensure this. Ament was well-established as an educator, world traveler (where he inspected collegiate and secondary schools throughout Europe), and philanthropist when he arrived in Forest Glen. He held a master's degree from Illinois State Normal University, an LL.D. from Transylvania University in Lexington, Kentucky, and a Ph.D. from Oskaloosa College and served as superintendent and president of several different colleges in the Midwest and Northeast. He later became director of the Silver Spring National Bank and the Columbia National Bank and was a charter member of the Congressional Country Club. He received knighthood in the Order of the Holy Sepulchre and the diploma of the Academic Internazionals. He was married to Teresa Catherine Welch of Howe Island, Canada. (Authors' collection.)

Surrounded by termini and seated on an ancient Greek bench, Dr. and Mrs. Ament, seated at right, confer with Dean Munford, center, after a tennis game. The bench and table are said to be ancient Greek and were located along the athletic fields; they were removed and their whereabouts are unknown. James Eli Ament arrived at NPS with a sterling reputation in education and a wealthy silent business partner, Joe Clifton Trees, the oil tycoon of Pennsylvania. Ament catered strictly to the daughters of the ultra-elite of the world, many of whom accompanied their fathers in embassy positions in Washington or were daughters from America's business and industrial giants. (Authors' collection.)

The Cassedys' creation of the physical campus was influenced by the architecture at the World's Columbian Exposition, where they purchased a book of plans from which nearly every building was designed. The World's Columbia Exposition influenced Ament, as well, who admired the "white city" style used there. In love with classicism, he commenced to stucco nearly all of the shingled buildings, often painting them white or a cream color. The Beaux-Arts style seemed to be coming of age in Forest Glen. Main, pictured here c. 1918, has been stripped of her foliage and given a fresh coat of stucco over shingle, with whitewash du-jour. (Authors' collection.)

This pen and ink, which predates the kitchen and dining addition to Main and the completion of the Odeon wings, was signed (illegibly) by an artist named Bailey. It clearly defines Ament's desire to interconnect all buildings, a process the Cassedys started in 1900. By 1927, nearly every building (with the exception of a few sororities and the Miller Library) were connected via covered walkways or causeways. The domed turret of the inn was cut in half with the addition of the ballroom link in 1921. The massive structure dwarfing Senior House is the Aments' home, the President's House. The Belvedere tower with open eaves, which stands 300 feet above sea level, was reconfigured to hold tubular chimes, a memorial gift from students. (Authors' collection.)

58

Many girls who had graduated under the Cassedys were concerned with Dr. Ament's changes. Nearly every building received an addition, whether for domestic purposes such as bath, kitchen, and living space or fanciful details such as the addition of hundreds of caryatids near the quadrangle. Ament traveled to war-torn Europe and purchased loads of statuary, some originals and some reproductions. Regardless, all were classic pieces, and some had substantial value. Here are NPS girls in and out of Main, mindless of the juxtaposition of shingle and stucco on the old inn, or the transition the NPS campus was making from rustic to Beaux Arts. (Authors' collection.)

The Forest Glen castle, seen here in another of its many lives, was converted into apartments by Dr. Ament for visiting families of students. The venture proved unsuccessful as most stayed in D.C. The improvements to the building are noteworthy, as the castle roof and center courtyard were additions he made almost exactly emulating his childhood home. (Library of Congress.)

The Dell, or Greensward, at National Park Seminary is the most important use of open land on the campus, especially today as the beltway has drastically reduced green space for concrete. Located just below the fountain circle, this Greensward was an important part of the inn as well, as patrons received their first introduction to the building through this approach. Here, NPS girls meander the Greensward on a fall day in 1923. (Authors' collection.)

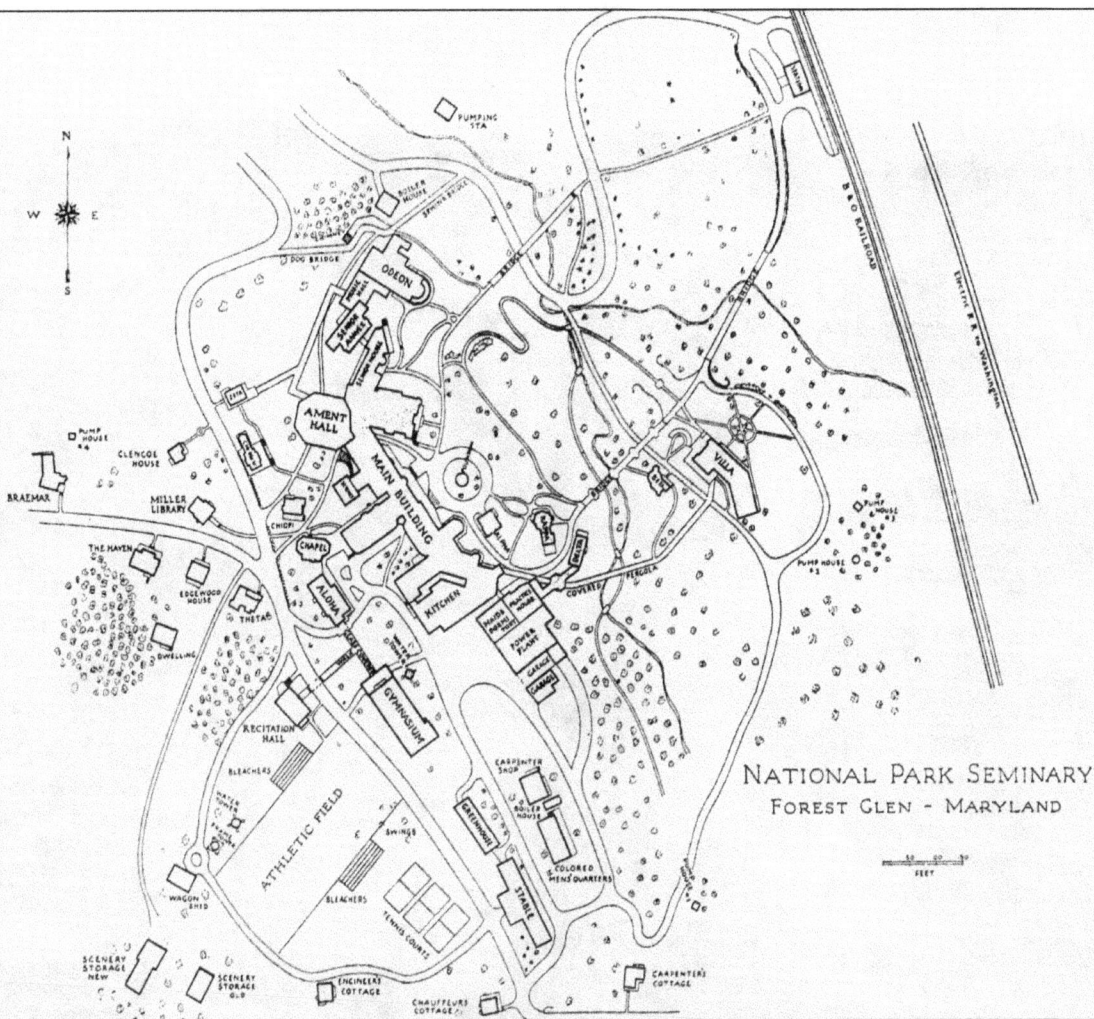

Additions and the building program complete, this map gives a general impression of NPS without showing the farm and acreage purchased by Ament in 1928. NPS at one time contained almost 300 acres, of which approximately 25 are seen here. Notice how many buildings are interconnected. (Authors' collection.)

Harley Nichols painted this image several times to add new buildings as the campus grew. This dates to 1930, and though some buildings are displaced because of the scale, it gives a general

idea of the complexity and beauty that was NPS in Forest Glen. (Authors' collection.)

Ament's crowning achievement was the completion of the Ament Hall, a ballroom built on a massive scale in 1921. It became the largest building in lower Montgomery County and inspired the Silver Spring Volunteer Fire Department to purchase their first hook-and-ladder truck. It was also an exclusive dormitory that catered to the ultra wealthy. The ballroom suites were designed for a double occupancy—a student and personal assistant or maid. Zeta, the Swiss chalet, stood on this site for many years and was moved west in 1921 to its current location to make room for the ballroom. (Authors' collection.)

NPS girls well portray the non–co-ed institution. Ballroom dance, shown in this image, was both an elective course and training for the more formal affairs, when middies from Annapolis or boyfriends from home came to NPS. The 42 plaster statues seen on the top level of the ballroom range in subject from Hiawatha to Christopher Columbus. (Authors' collection.)

Walls throughout the ballroom and other buildings at NPS were heavily decorated with hand-painted scenes, believed to have been done by students led by Louie Regal, a French artist specializing in such work. Here, students relax in wicker while being lulled by music from the NPS's massive Victor Auditorium Orthophonic Victrola. (Authors' collection.)

Senior Annex, seen to the right in 1936, was built in 1911. The English oak in front, planted by the Class of 1912, memorializes peace between the United States and Great Britain for 100 years after the War of 1812. To the left, rarely photographed, is the President's House, built in 1919 directly into the large front gable of Senior House. Most new buildings were constructed while the girls were home for summer recess. When they returned in the fall, the new structures were surprises, but President's House upset more girls than it surprised. Alums also protested its placement. Little could be done, and Dr. and Mrs. Ament lived there together until 1936. (Authors' collection.)

The whimsical pitch of the roof and the garden-like setting made the canoe house a fairly-tale place to store and launch canoes. Located on the western border of the campus, the canoe house stood until all traces were lost in flooding by 1973. Only ruins of the concrete ramp and metal gears of the cable winch remain today. The cleared land in the background is Edgewood's pasture, and the road is Ireland Drive. This photo dates to 1923. (Authors' collection.)

Sports competitions were weekly events between the east and west side sororities, athletic clubs, and neighboring schools. NPS had a champion basketball team for many years and competed with girls from such schools as George Washington University, Gallaudet University, University of Maryland, and Mount Vernon Seminary. All students were required to walk and document 100 miles a school year; many documented walking to McKeever's Ice Cream in Kensington. Every girl also had a daily gym period. Here, freshmen compete against each other in the 20-yard dash. Usually, a young army officer from nearby Walter Reed Hospital judged sporting and equestrian events; one is seen in the right foreground. (Authors' collection.)

Wigwagging in 1919 helped the girls better understand the rigors of World War I. Select students participated for a full semester in a mock army base named Camp Steever, complete with olive drab middies. Camps were set up near the rose garden and on the playing fields, seen here. Using signal flags, the girls learned semaphore wigwagging and other rigors of military life. Many spent weekends in tents. Girls not part of the camp knitted socks, which were shipped to American Expeditionary Forces through the Red Cross. (Authors' collection.)

In the hall leading to the ballroom link, built by Dr. Ament to connect Main with the ballroom, was the German bronze sculpture at left named the Amazon Group. It was a gift from the German chancellor to NPS. Also in this image is a fabulous Mercer tiled fireplace. All of NPS's fine antiques were long ago sold at auction, and mediocre information exists about their whereabouts. However, the fate of the Amazon Group is well-documented, as it, along with a massive and ancient Japanese lantern and many of NPS's massive ornamental iron gates, were part of the scrap drive after December 7, 1941. As such, it can be assumed the German bronze sculpture and Japanese iron lantern were each returned to their respective countries in a not-too-desirable form. (Authors' collection.)

The fountain in front of Main was purchased by Dr. Ament in Europe. It was alleged to be of Istrian marble and 700 years old, but this was later found to be incorrect. Regardless, it became the centerpiece of the front entrance to NPS. All of the horses' mouths spewed water, as did the putti on top. The pump house was located below the retaining wall nearby. Dismantled after World War II for repair, it is in disrepair today. (Authors' collection.)

For years, this marble sculpture was misidentified by NPS as the mythological figure Acteon. Actually of Cyporissus, it is one of many pieces bought by Dr. Ament and is said to have belonged to the Hopkins family of Baltimore. The students had their own name for it: oftentimes, when running down past Cyporissus on their way to catch a train at the station, the whistle would blow and the train would pull away, so they nicknamed it "My God I Missed The Train!" (Authors' collection.)

One of the most formal structures at NPS was the Odeon. Seen here after Ament's additions, it served the seminary as playhouse, theater, and host of nearly every baccalaureate Sunday. To the left of Odeon is Teresa Catherine Hall, a conservatory of music. To the right is the Scenery Wing, which via a system of hoists, pulleys, and tracks, housed the scenery backdrops for plays and performances. Greek statuary was located on the roof above each column of the wings. Most of the structure burned in 1993. (Authors' collection.)

At peak enrollment, NPS had almost 400 students with many on waiting lists. Most were boarders, but a few were day students. The lowest enrollment was just under 40 during the Depression. Pictured in the arts and crafts room are girls studying mechanical drawing and art. The Cassedys had many non-traditional methods of teaching that proved highly successful. "Soul power," or moral training, was a strong part of their early educational philosophy, and in the history of the women's education movement is scarcely seen today. (Authors' collection.)

Dorm rooms were everything from quaint single rooms to double-room suites with private baths. Prices were in the hundreds of dollars, and many girls were socially judged by where they lived on campus. There were six dormitories: Aloha, Villa, Senior House and Annex, Main, and the Ballroom. Students did not live in the sororities, and none are known to have lived off campus other than the day students. The room above, described as "one of the less expensive rooms," was typical of what most NPS girls experienced. (Authors' collection.)

Pictured is the 1919 NPS basketball team. The construction of the gym allowed the girls to practice and compete on a more collegiate level. In later years, NPS began accepting junior and senior high school girls as part of a four-year curriculum. Ultimately, NPS catered almost entirely to girls attending the last two years of high school and their first two years of college. Many went on to fully accredited colleges, while others simply married and lived off of their families' often extensive wealth. (Authors' collection.)

The Villa was for villains, or so Dean Munford thought, and she would regularly peer into dorm room windows to remind the girls that closed blinds were not a substitute for clean rooms. After several reminders, she had the blinds removed. In the late 1920s, the 1930s, and the 1940s, planes flew low over the Villa; rumors as to the reason was not substantiated until 1994, when a 100-year reunion was given on the grounds and an alum said that many girls sunbathed on the roof. Indeed, the authors purchased an NPS scrapbook from 1928 and found this image within. (Authors' collection.)

May Day celebration was an annual tradition, seen here taking place in front of Edgewood in 1931. In 1928, Dr. Ament purchased the Edgewood plantation from the Keys family, thus increasing NPS's land to over 200 acres. He renamed the farm Amentdale. NPS became self-sufficient, as the working farm produced pork, poultry, eggs, milk, cheese, and an array of vegetables. The Depression had many setbacks for NPS and came just after Dr. Ament bought Edgewood and another large home, the Oaks. Fortunately, by making the school self-sufficient, Ament kept the school afloat with help from the alumnae association. (Authors' collection.)

Dr. Ament's impact on NPS and the history of education is remarkable. His ideals for the teaching of young women, though now considered antiquated, catered to a unique socio-economic class hardly seen today. Interestingly, his ideals never really evolved from refining girls into womanhood, even during the Great Depression when education was needed to make a living. Dr. Ament passed away in 1936 after several illnesses and is buried at Rock Creek Cemetery near the Cassedys and Thomas Franklin Schneider. His dedicated wife took over presidency of NPS and continued the traditions established by the Cassedys. (Authors' collection.)

Members of the Class of 1937 work feverishly to produce NPS's annual yearbook, *The Acorn*. Seen here are Betty Webb, Esther Dickinson, Edith Geissler, Ruth Murray Cook, Dorthea Lockwood, Mary Louise Davis, Joan Sheridan, Betty Lou Skillman, Ruth Wheary, Naomi Ellisberg, Lenore Haucke, Geraldine Gillis, and Jane Campbell. America was full scale into the Depression when this image was taken, and many students and parents desired an education more geared towards making a living. (Authors' collection.)

Mrs. Teresa Catherine Ament, right, sits with, from left to right, 1937 senior class president Dorothy Porritt, junior president Camille Fuller, and sub-junior president Jean Owen. The students and alumnae essentially kept NPS open during the Depression by sending their daughters, cousins, nieces, friends, and any girl they could recruit to school in Forest Glen. In the 1930s, many students said their sisters, mothers, and aunts attended NPS. The burden of managing NPS as well as her husband's vast real estate and the Edgewood farm proved too much for Mrs. Ament, and by 1937, she decided to sell the school. (Authors' collection.)

A friend of the Aments, Roy Tasco Davis, met them while a page on Capitol Hill under Joseph Cannon, who called upon a constituent's daughter at NPS around 1920. Like Ament, Dr. Davis had an extensive background in education, having attended LaGrange College and Brown University. Davis managed Stephens College and served as a delegate to the Republican National Convention. In the 1920s and 1930s, he served as U.S. minister to Guatemala, Costa Rica, and Panama. He was married to Loyce Enloe, who, like him, hailed from Missouri. Dr. Davis assumed the mortgage on NPS; there are no records that he paid anything for it, but deeds stipulated he pay Mrs. Ament $15,000 per year until her death. An apartment once utilized by Joe Clifton Trees on the lower level of the ballroom was given to her as well. He immediately leased out the Edgewood farm and renamed the school National Park College (NPC). (Authors' collection.)

NPC stressed equestrian sports more than the seminary had, and nearly every girls participated. Many miles of trails leading into Rock Creek Park were heavily trotted, and seen here with a group of NPC girls in 1940 is Captain von Bretzel, NPC equitation instructor, a former Imperial Dragoon under the czar of Russia. During Dr. Davis's reign, NPC was soon chartered as a junior college, and while many of the old traditions of the seminary were kept, modern changes adapted the school and the girls to the working world. (Authors' collection.)

Seven NPC girls stopped to enjoy the rebirth of the woods in Forest Glen in spring 1940. The stop is along one of the many bridges on Ireland Drive leading down to the canoe house on Rock Creek and the picnic house. The road had been an old farm trail, used long ago to roll hogsheads of tobacco down to Rock Creek, where they were floated to Georgetown for trade. The paved road today is enjoyed by a magnitude of hikers and bikers on their way to and from Rock Creek Park. (Authors' collection.)

Despite all the changes at National Park, two traditions could always be relied upon: Halloween in the Glen and a letter delivered by Charles the postman. From the day the school opened until its last, Charles Leon Bullock was the postman, baggagemaster, and sympathetic ear of all National Park girls, giving advice or lending a hand. Well admired and always remembered, Mr. Bullock lived in D.C. but was given a home on campus by the Cassedys. (Save Our Seminary.)

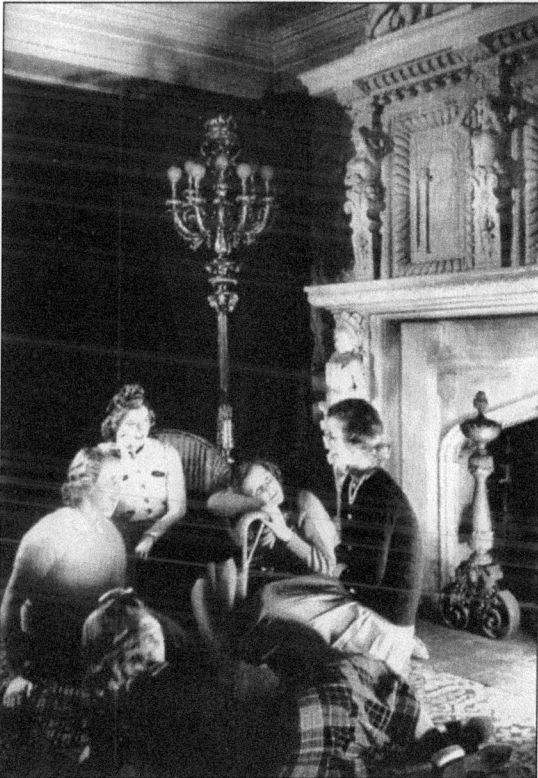

Liberated of uniforms, white gloves, and chaperones, NPC girls relax in front the massive ballroom fireplace installed by Dr. Ament. Once described as being like "when the Wizard of Oz goes from black and white to color," many NPC girls were ecstatic about the new ideals under Dr. Davis and could not even imagine living under the strict rules the alums had to endure. It seemed NPC was on track to recovery, thanks in part to continued support from the alums. Still, many alums were weary of change, and to quell any fears, Dr. Davis also agreed to maintain many of the old traditions and social and moral training established by the Cassedys. (Authors' collection.)

Though going co-ed was never an issue, dances and social gatherings both on and off campus became weekly events with the new administration. After all, Dr. Davis had once been president of Stephens College, a school nicknamed "the spouse trap," as nearly all his students married just after graduation. Travel to the Caribbean was also part of the NPC curriculum, as Davis had a sterling reputation with many Caribbean nations. In this photo of a formal dance in the ballroom in 1941, the original Victor Talking Machine Company's tapestry screen in front of the Orthophonic speaker is visible on the second level. (Authors' collection.)

NATIONAL PARK COLLEGE

SUCCESSOR TO NATIONAL PARK SEMINARY

FOREST GLEN, MARYLAND

SUBURB OF WASHINGTON, D.C.

ROY TASCO DAVIS
PRESIDENT

September 22, 1942

To Alumnae and Former Students of National Park College:

When a nation is fighting for its very existence, it is necessary for its Government to draft institutions as well as individuals for war emergency purposes. In the crisis that now confronts our Nation, men and women have been called from practically every home in the land to serve their country. Educational institutions have also been called to serve their country.

I deeply regret to inform you that the United States Government has found it necessary to take title by condemnation proceedings in the Federal Court to our entire National Park College property, for the use of the United States Army as a hospital. The fact that the campus and buildings are near Walter Reed Hospital Army Medical Centre makes them desirable and necessary for the use of the Government in the war emergency.

Under the circumstances there is nothing we can do but accept the Government's decision and make this sacrifice for the welfare of our country. I know that this will come as a shock to you, as it has to us, but I hope that you will feel that the sacrifice is not too great when you realize that the College will house the sick and the wounded who are fighting for democracy.

Since the Government has taken title to the property, it is not possible to make any plans for the future. However, I know that those who lived at and loved National Park will treasure memories of the days they spent here. I hope that the ideals and traditions of National Park which were developed and maintained by administrative officers, faculty and students during its long and useful service as an educational institution will guide and strengthen all of us in these trying times.

I shall find a place to safeguard the College records and make them available to those who may need transcripts of their grades in future years. I hope that the alumnae clubs will continue to maintain their organizations.

I am

Yours very sincerely,

Roy Tasco Davis

Roy Tasco Davis

NPC was short lived. This letter was circulated to all students, employees, and alums on September 22, 1942. Dozens of schools, hotels, and sanitariums were taken by the federal government for recuperating hospitals during the war emergency. Disappointed, many visited the old campus, saw the recuperating soldiers, and understood. Later, talk abounded about re-opening the school at another campus, but none could match the old and the army was unwilling to negotiate any sale to re-open the school. For two days, Weschlers Auction House of Washington sold all of the buildings' contents. Dr. Davis was paid $855,000 for the campus and Edgewood farm. NPS and NPC now belonged to the ages. (Authors' collection.)

NPC was to be immediately reopened as Walter Reed Army Hospital Forest Glen Annex, a recuperation hospital for wounded U.S. soldiers. Within six months, the first patients arrived and in many cases were reminded of the European front because of the architecture. This painting documented on canvas in 1944 by WPA artist Jack McMillan that the army was here to stay. Unfortunately, the image is a bit glorified as it shows no amputees or other difficulties faced by soldiers. The painting has been restored and hangs in the National Museum of Health and Medicine at Walter Reed Army Medical Center in Washington, D.C. (U.S. Army.)

Though the trolley had not stopped in Forest Glen since 1926, here is Capital Transit car 1100, a half cut version of a D.C. streetcar complete with steps and seating. The idea was to give amputees the opportunity to relearn basic skills—such as boarding transportation—before returning to society. To the right is president of Capital Transit Edward B. Merrill, who presented the trolley to the army in 1946. It sat in the vicinity of the recitation house on Linden Lane.

Three fellows model their new prosthetics while taking a smoke break next to the fountain in 1943. Rest and relaxation was the plan at the "Holiday Inn," as many solders called Main. Actually, all buildings had their names changed, mostly to numbers or wards: Main became Building 101, the Odeon Building 104, and the Dining Room the Chow Hall. Interior decorative elements were removed, nearly all exposed woodwork was painted lime green and yellow, and coffered ceilings were covered with tile or drop ceilings. Ornate lights were replaced with fluorescent lamps, while rooms were divided. The Odeon was gutted for a workshop and army band headquarters, the gym was retrofitted into a movie theater, and the ballroom was given an enormous stage. Recitation House was felled because of termites and, like the rose garden and greenhouse, to make way for cinder-block offices. (Save Our Seminary.)

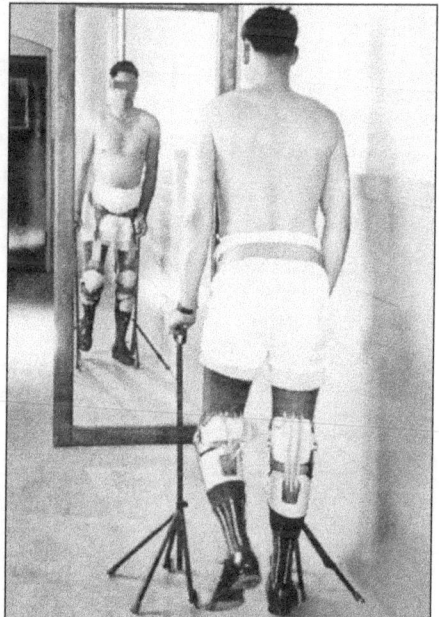

One of thousands needing rehab during World War II, this soldier has lost both legs but is learning to walk again. Some of the worst amputations, burns, and disfiguring injuries were seen at the Army Prosthesis Lab in Forest Glen. Forest Glen also included dental and facial repair. In later years, some patients in Forest Glen suffered shell shock or mental trauma. Many had never been exposed to castles and Tudor architecture except in the horror movies of the 1950s. To them, the place seemed weird and haunted and reminded them of the older generation who created such a place and the political outfalls that sent them to war. (National Medical Museum.)

The east side of campus had changed very little by winter 1945 when this image was taken, and the army was using every ounce of space. A few buildings were later lost: Edgewood was burned to make way for the Forest Glen Commissary; Recitation House, once known as Chapter House, was demolished because of termite damage; all slave cabins were destroyed; the Odeon and Scenery Wing were lost in a fire; and several out-buildings including the greenhouse were also demolished. The formal rose garden was leveled for a cinder-block office building, but many of the roses were transplanted at the main post of Walter Reed Army Medical Center. A walk there also yields many large urns and statuary, some of which are likely from Forest Glen. (Authors' collection.)

LAST DAY COVER

The Last Mail from

ғorest Glen, Montgomery County, Maryland

POST OFFICE DISCONTINUED

Frank P. Frey, Actg. P.M.

The U.S. Post Office, which had been in operation for many years across from the train station in the castle, closed in 1943 and re-opened a substation in Building 101 for the convenience of the wounded soldiers. This postcard was one of the few mailed from there on the last day, which was representative of what would soon come of the railroad station, the castle, and ultimately the old campus. (Authors' collection.)

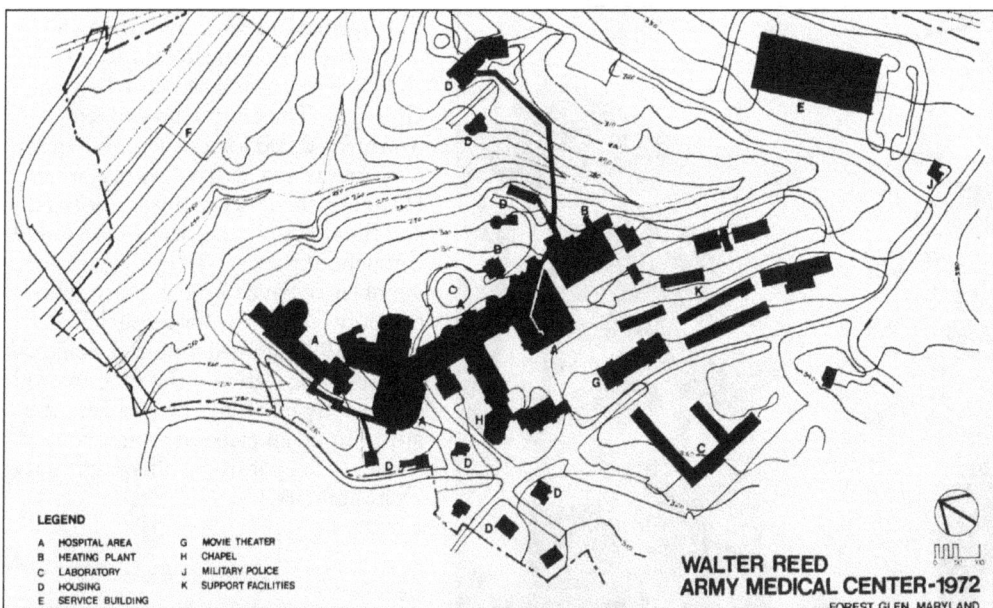

LEGEND

A	HOSPITAL AREA	G	MOVIE THEATER
B	HEATING PLANT	H	CHAPEL
C	LABORATORY	J	MILITARY POLICE
D	HOUSING	K	SUPPORT FACILITIES
E	SERVICE BUILDING		

WALTER REED
ARMY MEDICAL CENTER-1972
FOREST GLEN, MARYLAND

A stark contrast to the maps of Forest Glen created by NPS, this army map relates the loss of most of the bridges, construction of cinder-block office buildings, and the beltway arrival in the early 1960s. One of the largest bridges on campus had been the Sphinx Bridge, located just north of the Odeon, which today has been replaced by the Linden Lane Bridge over the beltway. Arrival of the beltway also destroyed the entrance road leading into the front of the site. (Authors' collection.)

Much structural damage occurred to the site between 1955 and 1975, when a lack of maintenance funding and the condition of the structures began to take their toll. Some patients played on the unusual site much as they would at Coney Island, often causing damage. Storms took their toll as well. The bell tower of the old inn fell during a hurricane in the 1960s. The cast-iron Honeysuckle Bridge shuttered and vibrated when patients and neighborhood children rode their bikes over it and was later demolished. The Main Drive Bridge or Castle Bridge, seen above, had its wooden road paved over for army use, which ultimately caused it to collapse inwards. In 1972, most of NPS was listed on the National Register of Historic Places after being threatened with demolition by the army. Save Our Seminary (SOS) was founded in 1988 to help preserve the site and guide its future. (Save Our Seminary.)

85

The gymnasium was converted to a movie theater during World War II and back to a gym during the Persian Gulf War. The army appropriated nearly $100,000 for a new gym floor for patients and active duty personnel. However, the leaky roof was not fixed, and hundreds of other leaks were found throughout the campus by vigilant members of Save Our Seminary, who petitioned the army for repairs. The gym in 1990 suffered serious damage from pooling water on the roof. Instead of correctly repairing the problem, the army put up an elaborate system of trusses to keep it from collapsing. (Save Our Seminary.)

By the end of the Vietnam War, few patients remained at Forest Glen, as a new hospital had been built at the main post of Walter Reed. These thee patients are descending the lion steps in front of Main around 1970. A decade later, most buildings were vacant or used for offices and storage. Seven of the eight sororities were used for officer housing, the exception being Beta's castle, which had suffered significant water damage from roof leaks. (Authors' collection.)

Controversy took place about the location of the Capital Beltway during planning in the early 1960s. A ride up Connecticut Avenue today just north of Randolph Road bears scars from where the above section of the beltway was supposed to be put in. Unfortunately, it ended up coming through Forest Glen. This massive cut is the beltway being installed. The arch to the Honeysuckle Bridge is in the foreground, and the castle and former site of the train station are also visible. (Save Our Seminary.)

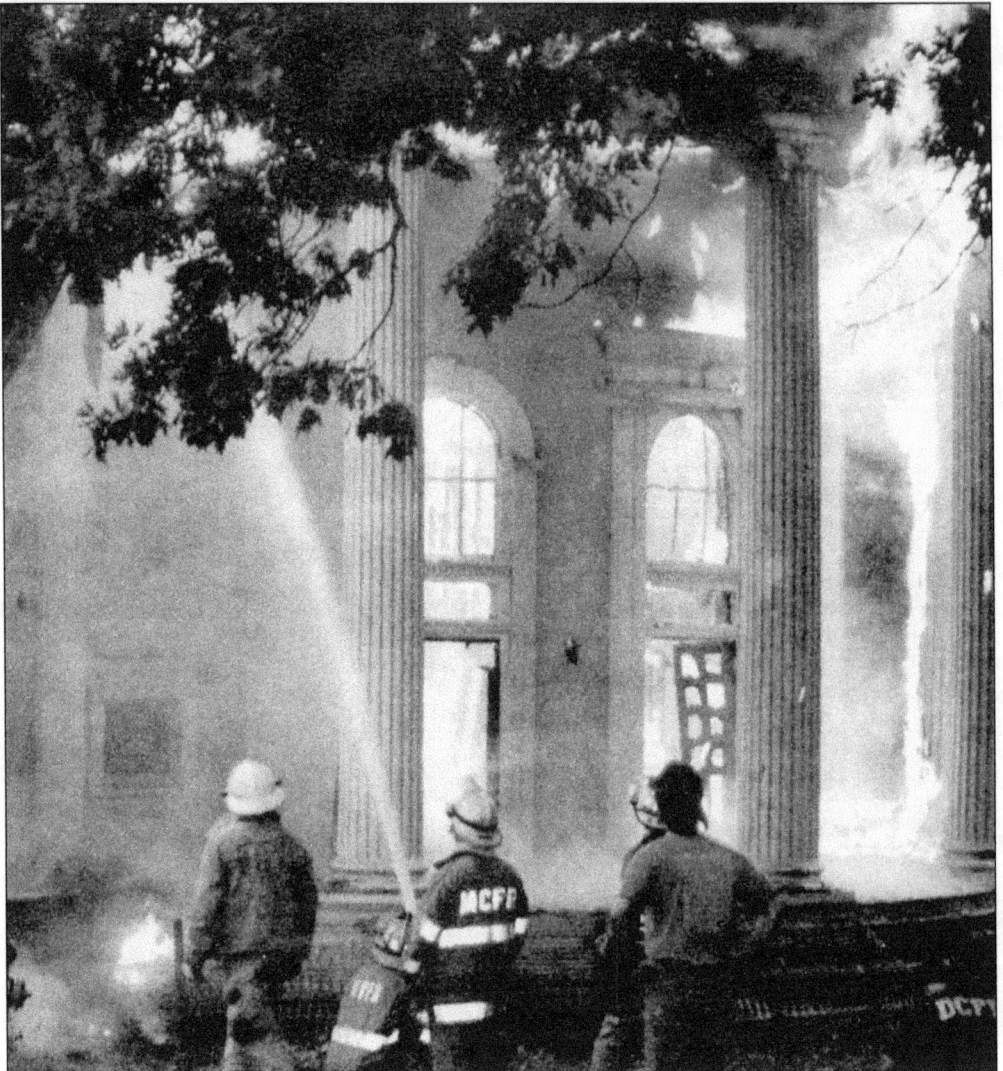

The loss of the Odeon to fire in 1993 brought about the end of an era. Everyone in the neighborhood was sick of the poor management, lack of maintenance, and inadequate security on the site. This fire was the last straw, prompting Save Our Seminary to file a demolition by neglect suit against the army the following year. Settled out of court, this was one of three major victories for SOS, which twice in the past prevented the site's demolition for army housing. (Save Our Seminary.)

Three

EIGHTY YEARS LATER

Hand-painted muses once lined the entire ceiling of the Odeon, but these were the last four in existence before the Odeon burned down. Much has been lost on the old NPS campus through the years. As this book goes to press, residents are on the verge of a new life in Forest Glen: The Alexander Company prepares to restore many of the old buildings into new homes and condos. This chapter gives an idea of the current conditions of some of the buildings and takes us back to see how they once were. (Authors' collection.)

This structure has been known as Ye Forest Inne, Main, and Building 101. By any name, it is the most important structure both architecturally and historically on the site. It is one of the last examples of Victorian resort architecture in the region, and though a little worse for the wear, missing her Belvedere tower, and in need of some manicure work, the old building is still the crowning gem of the neighborhood. (Authors' collection.)

Like two bookends, Cleo and Leo—sometimes know as Theo—stand guard over the stairs leading to the glen walk. The lions are of pot metal, painted by the army to look bronze. Damage was incurred as thieves tried to remove the lions, which were therefore cemented in place several years ago. The porch of Alpha is seen at right, as is that of Kappa to the rear. The bench was stolen in 1995. (Authors' collection.)

One of the most visually impressive buildings on the campus is the gymnasium, built in 1907 as a Greek temple. The glass-covered walkway supported by caryatids seen extending from the front columns led to Aloha and Recitation House. The walkway and Recitation House were demolished by the army. (Authors' collection.)

One of the most relaxing places on the campus, especially on a hot day when a mist sprayed, was the fountain at Main. Dr. Ament copied this from the inner court of a Venetian palace during one of his trips to Europe. Much of the fountain was disassembled for repair by the army after World War II. Two horses' heads were broken off by vandals over the past several decades. (Authors' collection.)

Today, most people think of the Metro Train Station near Georgia Avenue when someone mentions Forest Glen train station. However, this old station was designed and built by B&O architect E.F. Baldwin in 1887. The iron fence between the tracks discouraged people from crossing. The preferred crossing method was via a tunnel under the tracks between the station and the glass-covered building and waiting shelter at right. The above image dates to 1925. The station was demolished in 1955 and the tracks slightly moved when the beltway was built in the mid-1960s. (Authors' collection.)

Undoubtedly the most picturesque bridge on campus was the iron Walk Bridge, built in 1887 by the Forest Glen Improvement Company. By the time the beltway was built, this was the last bridge standing, although it was soon after demolished. As a child, author Ric Nelson recalls riding his bike onto the bridge where the wooden planks and the vibration of the iron trusses made an awful racket. The wooden planks were replaced three times during the bridge's life; photographs can be dated based on the direction the boards were laid. The above photograph is c. 1920. Below, NPS buff Bill McNinn stands next to the bridge entranceway, cleared of nearly 50 years of growth and debris by him, exposing the stone buttresses and trails. (Authors' collection.)

The Odeon was the first building constructed on campus using stucco rather than shingle. Perhaps it was the popular style at the time, or perhaps it simulated masonry in a building electrified by a fire-prone technology. Regardless, it was one of the most important buildings on the campus aesthetically and historically and was lost to an arson fire in 1993. The massive firewall, several of which were built by the army in the 1940s, essentially saved the rest of the buildings. (Authors' collection.)

Linden Lane is seen looking north towards Woodstock Avenue in 1906 (above) and again in 1930 (below). Notice that Recitation House was originally located in front of the gym and was moved across the street by Dr. Ament to complete the gym's front porch. The brick arch was part of the elaborate glass-covered caryatid walkway. An oversized truck demolished the arch, and later, the army removed the rest. (Authors' collection.)

Recitation House was originally built in 1900 as Chapter or Mother Sorority House for sororities that did not yet have a house. The building was divided into four large rooms and after all sororities were built was used for classroom space and moved across the street. It was demolished by the army because of termite damage. (Authors' collection.)

One of the many scenic nooks on the grounds was this view from Practice House towards Kappa. The wonderful old columns had originally been purchased for construction of a Roman Triumphal Arch over the road in the foreground, but that idea was scratched as the campus topography and location of Kappa prevented it. Instead, the Roman arch was redesigned as the building seen at right, the Delta Colonial house, and the columns placed in front of Practice House. (Authors' collection.)

Below the ballroom was this beautiful courtyard, where the rear of Senior House, the Chateau Garden Causeway, and the Teresa Catherine Hall all came together. The road led from Linden Lane, past the pagoda, under the ballroom, past the Dog Bridge, and across the Sphinx Bridge to the train station. The causeway, one of several covered walks around the campus, connected the ballroom with Zeta's Swiss chalet, Senior House, and Teresa Catherine Hall. The ballroom porch was removed by the army, and the brick structure is an army fire escape. The above image dates to about 1924. (Authors' collection.)

The Chateau Garden Causeway is an important architectural feature to the site built on a large, formal garden scale. It serves as a medieval buffer between the typical, post-war architecture of the neighborhood and the eclectic collection on the other side. Though boarded up, the structure is stable and worthy of restoration. The above image dates to 1924 during the heyday of NPS. (Authors' collection.)

The original stables built by the Forest Glen Improvement Company burned down in 1910, and the new stables, seen above, were built the following year. The eagle was destroyed around 1983, probably by vandals, and pieces of it are stored in the basement of Main. Today, the stables are used as a transitional shelter for homeless men through Catholic charities. (Authors' collection.)

The tennis courts, seen here in 1918, dated back to the inn and remained a favorite at NPS and NPC. They were removed by the army for a parking lot and cinder-block office buildings by 1955. Linden Lane and the gymnasium are seen in the rear. (Authors' collection.)

A favorite pastime was the boat swings. Located next to the athletic fields, they stood from about 1923 until removed by the army. These were an old standard at amusement parks and playgrounds throughout the United States at the time. The gazebo overlooking the athletic fields was built by NPS's carpentry shop on top of the stumps of two trees. (Authors' collection.)

The Main Drive Bridge, also known as Castle Bridge, was made of stucco over wood framing shortly after the Cassedys purchased the site. Though capable of carrying horses, buggies, and early automobiles, it was not designed to carry heavy army trucks no matter how much asphalt was poured on top. It collapsed onto itself in the 1960s. The above image was taken in 1919. In the bottom photo, the tower of Beta's castle is seen on the top left. (Authors' collection.)

The colossal statue of justice was one of three multi-ton, cast-concrete statues located in vicinity of the Villa. Though she was purchased by the Cassedys, her dated pedestal is of another era and was most likely purchased at auction and moved to NPS around 1909. Her once formal gardens extended from the Villa to the "Y" in the glen where the two streams meet. Though she has seen better days, it is interesting to walk through the area and see both ruins and remnants of gardens and bridges. Her scale and sword were broken off sometime after 1942. (Authors' collection.)

A dormitory used mostly by sophomores, this was one of the best examples of an Italian villa in the region if not on the East Coast. The Cassedys did not feel the structure was complete even though the girls had moved in by 1908. A true villa had to have gardens, and by 1909, most of the surrounding gardens were completed and the Villa officially dedicated. The above image dates to 1910. Today, the building is boarded up but structurally sound, having recently served as bachelor enlisted quarters for the army. (Authors' collection.)

Between the Villa and railroad tracks was the small Minerva Gardens. Named after the Greek goddess of mechanical arts, Minerva, seen in the center, is over 10 feet tall and made of cast concrete. Silva, another goddess of similar size, is located on the other side of the Villa. The caduceus she carries is also a symbol used by the U.S. Army Medical Department, so she was well-dressed for the duration of that era. Though darkened today from years of steam trains and beltway emissions, she is as majestic as ever and with vigilance awaits the new occupant. The trucks are army storage. (Authors' collection.)

The importance of secluding the seniors from the rest of the students could not be stressed enough by the Cassedys. Seniors were products of NPS (and later, NPC) and as such were treated special. Architecturally, Senior House was one of those dorms in which many students dreamed of living. Its interiors were large and posh, and most important was the center parlor, which was fed by each corridor and room. Here, informal gatherings took place at any hour of the day or night. Senior House was the only structure to use Seneca sandstone in its foundation. The brick structure to the right below is an army fire escape. (Authors' collection.)

Porches were added to Senior House during Dr. Ament's administration, as well as a hooded window and second gable with unique wave shingle pattern. Added to the rear of this building was Senior Annex, built to accommodate increasing class sizes. Many plaques are seen in front of Senior House, memorializing graduating classes who planted ivy, which represents eternity, from different parts of the world. All of it has been removed by the army. (Authors' collection.)

Aloha was built by the Cassedys as their home in Forest Glen, but it quickly evolved into a dorm for freshmen as the Cassedys wanted to keep a close eye on them! It is the small bungalow structure seen to the far right in this image. Dr. Ament added on the caryatid walkways. Though boarded up, the building is in good condition and will likely become co-ops when restored. The large structure to the right of the oak tree is an army fire escape painted white. (Authors' collection.)

A whimsical little spot and favorite destination, the old picnic house on the banks of Minihaha Creek is found along the bridle path or "Ireland Drive," leading up from Rock Creek Park. A fence installed by the army restricts people from entering into Walter Reed. Designed by the NPS student seen standing next to the upper roaster facing the camera, the site is likely the former spot of a springhouse or mill used by the Edgewood farm. Today, though looking like Mayan ruins, the building is structurally sound. However, its surroundings suffer years of poorly planned drainage, new road grading, a lack of maintenance, and loss of the bridge crossing Minihaha Creek. The wooden roof also needs replacing. (Authors' collection.)

Probably no other corridor in NPS so reminded the girls of home than the approach and smell of food coming from the dining room, seen here in 1924. Though NPS's dining room evolved from the inn and was expanded from seating for 100 to 1,000 during the army era, it always kept its home-like charm and was used from 1887 until 1974. The archways, woodwork, and stained glass were removed around 1944. (Authors' collection.)

The Cassedys claimed to own the largest collection of Chippendale chairs known to exist in the world. Though reproductions, they would be valued at around $400 each today. Weschlers and Sons Auction House sold all after the army take-over. The army kept the school's silverware. The interior woodwork is painted white, yellow, and lime green, and acoustic tiles have replaced the wooden ceilings. The fireplace was covered up to protect it from thieves and vandals who became indigenous to the site after the army began deferring maintenance and security, especially in the 1990s. (Authors' collection.)

The Rear Courtyard, or Quadrangle, was the back door of Main, but since the Capital Beltway caused removal of the entrance bridges, passersby don't even know the other side exists! In this image taken in fall of 1922, the West Wing is to the left, and the addition to the kitchen is to the right, where Ye Bluebird was located. Today the entire rear is paved over. (Authors' collection.)

The Main Entrance Parlor was a favorite stop for the girls and certainly a place that left an image on visitors' minds. It remained practically the same from 1887 until 1942, when all furnishings were sold and the fretwork, arches, wooden stairways, and stained glass were removed for an environment more in style with contemporary tastes and requiring less maintenance. The fireplace was partially removed by thieves in 2002 and boarded up for security. (Authors' collection.)

The beautiful corridor known as Ballroom Link was built in anticipation of the ballroom in 1920. The corridor extends past the Mercer tiled fireplace that marks the terminus of the original inn. To the left is the Amazon Group in bronze. The thick carpet is a deep ox-blood red that became legend in later years. Most of the damage seen is cosmetic, caused by leaky heat pipes. The original wainscoting remains but has been painted yellow. (Authors' collection.)

Some dance in the ballroom in 1924, while others relax and listen to music from the school's Orthophonic Victrola, pictured center. The army installed a stage in the ballroom to host USO shows, and many big names played there. The immense size of the ballroom, which was named Ament Hall, creates wonderful acoustics and a spectacular light show in the evening as the sun sets against the massive stained-glass dormers and shadows are thrown from the clerestory ceiling. Today, the hall is in excellent condition but in need of cosmetic work, and many people look forward to future public dances being held there. (Authors' collection.)

The main parlor at Senior House was the place where friendships were made for an eternity. It was a place where seniors could come any time and find someone to talk to or just relax by the fireplace. It was centrally located in the building so nearly all rooms and halls fed into it. Today, it serves as an example of what happens to a building when maintenance is deferred and the property owners turn a deaf ear to the pleas of preservationists. (Authors' collection.)

Reading letters from home in the cupola of the Chateau Garden Causeway in 1922, these girls probably didn't even notice the beautiful rug beneath their feet as they fumbled to sit, open, and read in what was usually the most anticipated event of the day. Though stable today, the causeway, like many other buildings, is in need of some cosmetic work. The pipes are an army-added heat system and standpipe. (Authors' collection.)

At the Washington's Birthday Ball, an annual rite held at NPS and NPC nearly every year, a group of NPS girls in 1925 are extravagantly dressed for the occasion. They stand in the ballroom next to the old French fireplace in the rear of the building. NPS owned an enormous collection of costumes that were donated to the school and stored in the Odeon. The fireplace today, which is of plaster, is in very good condition. (Authors' collection.)

The proscenium arch was the main feature of the Odeon, and in its center was this massive face bust of an unknown Greek goddess, which had been one of the most revered statuary at NPS. For nearly half a century, she peered down upon performers on the Odeon's stage. This is the only known image of her. Her face had a quieting effect on the audience, and her smile was compared to that of Mona Lisa. Her love was for NPS, as the army removed her balconies and orchestra pit, demolished her stage, and gutted her seating for two floors of workshops. Still, the proscenium arch survived, but only as a broken and divided clue to a play from long ago. Perhaps she could take no more and was soon after lost in the great fire of 1994. The author took the above image in 1988, standing on the second floor just three feet below what at one time was the Odeon's 40-foot proscenium arch. (Authors' collection.)

Four

SURVIVING THE
UNITED STATES ARMY

Our neighborhood has suffered an identity crisis for many years. Although named Forest Glen Park, one wouldn't know it based on the number of U.S. Army signs that have warned of random searches and prosecuting trespassers since 1942. It was a sad day when NPC was closed by the army, but that is about to change. As the army pulls out of the historic district, they will leave behind nearly all the buildings taken during World War II. They will keep most of the old Edgewood pastures, where government buildings have since been built and where they are planning 300 new units of military housing. They will also begin using the city name of Silver Spring, giving us back the name Forest Glen Park. (Authors' collection.)

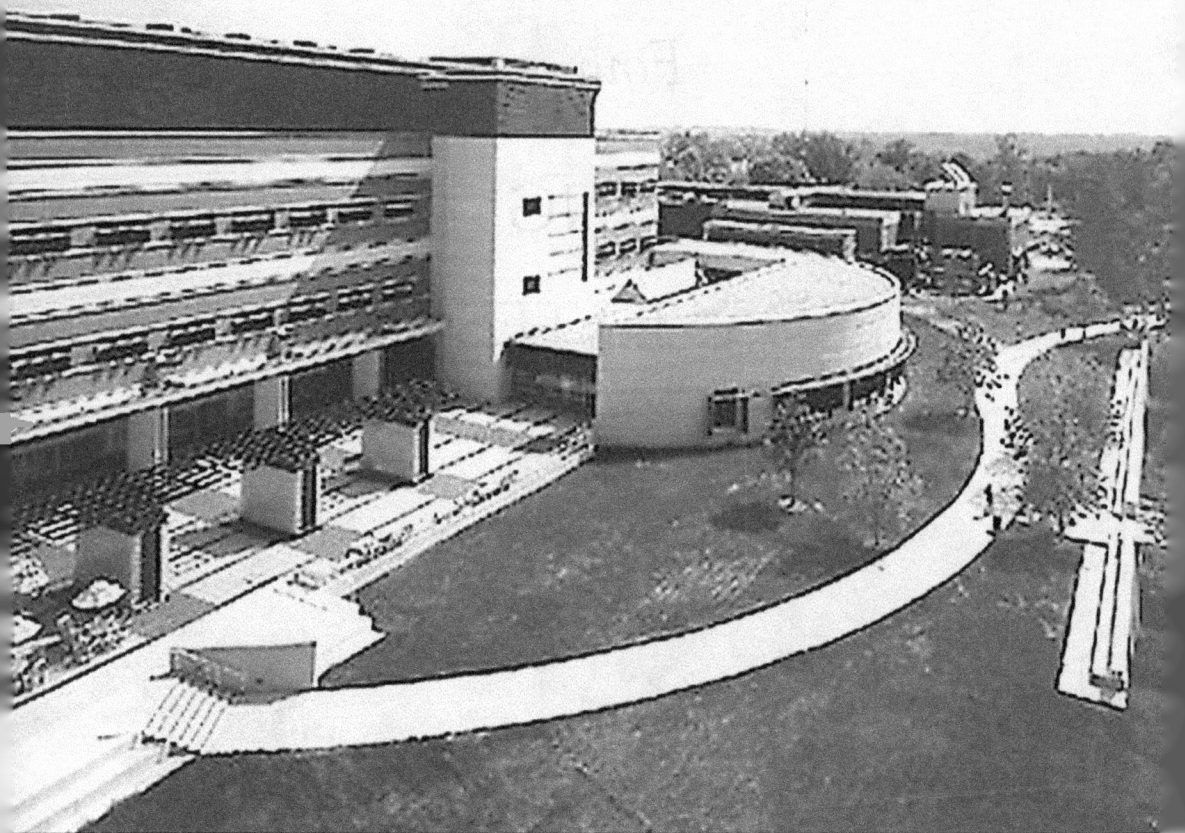

Perhaps the safest place to handle anthrax, dengue, and malaria, Walter Reed Army Institute of Research is an exceptional place with capable people working to ensure a safer tomorrow. The Daniel K. Inouye building was constructed on former Edgewood tobacco fields. The patio and umbrella in the lower left corner stand about 100 feet from one of the old hewn-log cabins believed to have housed Edgewood slaves. The radio tower in the distance is from the old WOL site, which now belongs to WWDC, known locally as DC 101. Much of that property belonged to the Ray family and was sold after World War II. Following an imaginary line along the road leading off to the right is the now defunct nuclear reactor, believed to be cold, constructed by the army decades ago. (Walter Reed Army Institute of Research.)

Postmaster Charles Bullock was given full use of this brick house as a gift for his many years of service to NPS and NPC. At one time, this building had an enormous tank where carbon was added to water to make gas for lighting on the grounds. Dating to the inn, it was gutted for use as a residence by 1910 when NPS was electrified. The house in the background fronts Woodstock Avenue; named Edgewood II by Dr. Ament, it is a Sears catalog home. Both were army property and are scheduled for restoration. The road in front is Woodstock Court, one of the last multi-home developments in the community. (Authors' collection.)

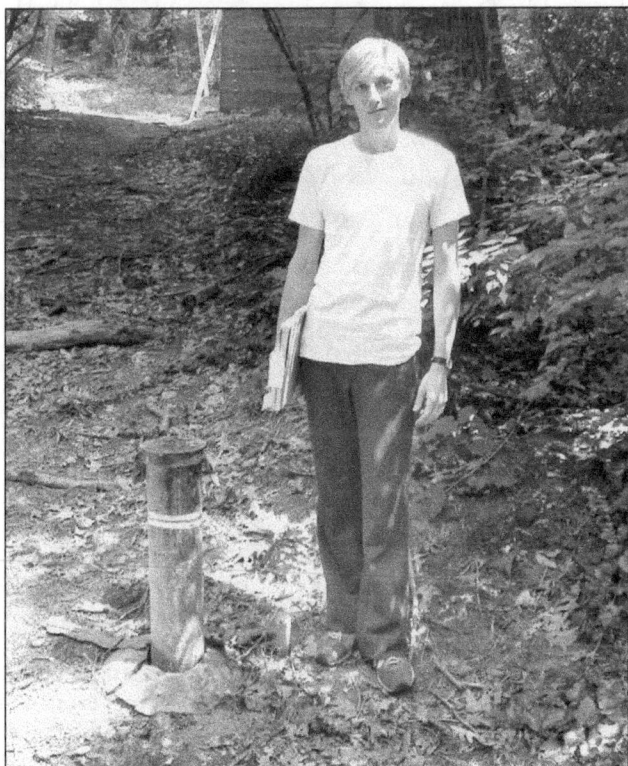

Resident Kevin Buckholdt stands by a core sample dug by the army to test the earth for contaminants. Core samples were taken for many years around the historic district as well, as radiation and other hazardous substances used in medicine and research were stored there. Much of the park around Ireland Drive was transferred to Maryland National Capital Park and Planning Commission over the past several years. The old path today is covered by a canopy created by different species of trees. (Authors' collection.)

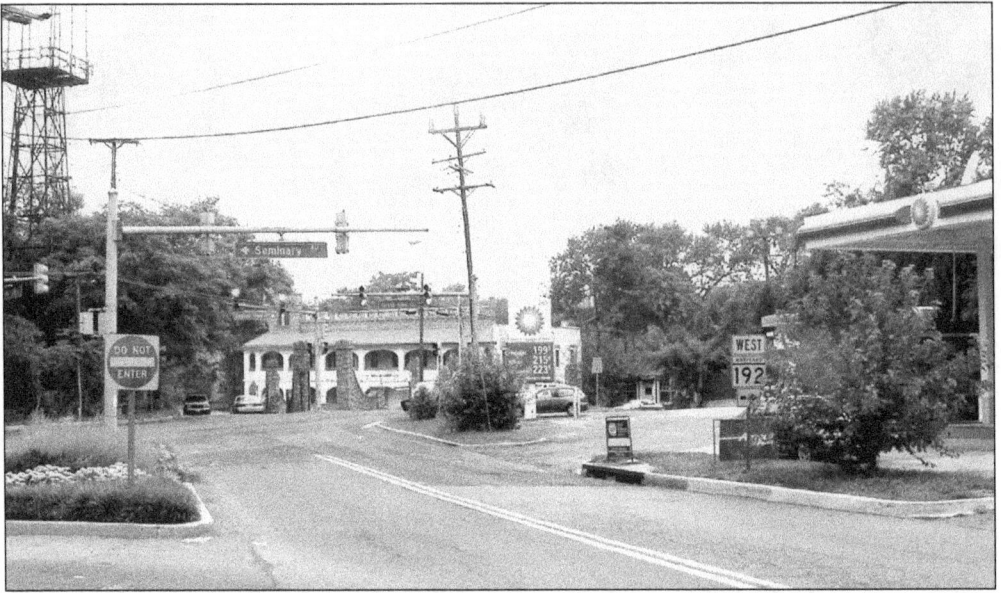

A busy intersection today, Forest Glen Road was a dirt path and Seminary Road a dirt grading for the streetcar tracks a century ago. The Glen Manor Hotel, which was entered from Glen Avenue, stood near the location of the gas station. A short-lived venture similar to Ye Forest Inne, it was demolished. A trolley waiting station and band shell stood behind the gas station for many years as well. The trolley tracks dead-ended on the other side of Seminary Road, where the conductor walked to the back of the car for the return trip to Washington. The stone courtyard, designed by Dr. Ament, is today a parking lot. Visible through the trees is the Forest Glen Country Store, originally Fowlers Store and later a store and restaurant. The tower seen at left was an army-installed lookout post and air raid siren from World War II. (Authors' collection.)

Forest Glen has a rich tradition of being architecturally diverse. Even mediocre, bland, and unimaginative styles are an important part of our heritage. The Forest Glen Metro Station is located at the corner of Georgia Avenue and Forest Glen Road. Interestingly, the natural springs in this region were an asset to early settlers and the Carroll Springs Inn but a headache for Metro planners. The Forest Glen Metro tunnel is one of the deepest in the world because of the complexity of the water table and underground springs. Even today, water trickles around the waiting platform, and stalactites are seen forming from ceilings. (Authors' collection.)

A local landmark for many years, the Keys descendants built this house and barn in the triangular lot bounded by Warren Street, Brookeville Road, and Montgomery Street. When the last of the Keys moved from the area c. 1985, the property was sold, buildings demolished, and new homes constructed by 1990. The house was of solid granite and, like its neighbor in Forest Glen Park, the Haven, which was built the same year and is a similar bungalow, the walls were 20 inches think. The barn was likely earlier vintage as the Keys property extended to this area. It was also the last farm barn of this type in lower Montgomery County. The authors surveyed the property and took these pictures prior to demolition, c. 1989. The barn was full of farming equipment, and the house in very good condition. A large marble plaque once located on the outside of the house read "ENOS C. KEYS BUILT 1907" and was last seen sitting like a trophy in the office of the developer. (Authors' collection.)

Montgomery Street crossed the tracks and connected to the Edgewood house, located 200 yards west of the old Linden B&O station. Named "Dilles addition to Linden," this area was the first suburban community developed with the arrival of the B&O Railroad in 1873. The Keys family owned the property and renamed the main thoroughfare from Ray's Road to Dilles Road, which is today Linden Lane. The structure at right is the old Linden Town Hall and E.C. Keys General Store, later George Wolfe's General Store. The Keys owned the warehouse behind it and sold it to the county as the liquor control warehouse. Soon moved to the old Ray property, the warehouse now belongs to a roofing company. Francis Wolfe, a longtime local resident, recalled the Keys sprucing up the community with the addition of wooden sidewalks. Within a year, people were back walking in the street as bees moved into the sidewalks! (Authors' collection.)

Looking northeast near Forest Glen today, it is hard to believe Brookeville Road dates to Colonial times. Not long ago, Lyttonsville thrived here. Many residents were freed slaves from neighboring plantations. Lyttonsville fell into disrepair by the 1930s. In 1951, the state adopted a commercial zoning plan for area, and in 1955, a survey said all homes were sub-standard, most did not have electricity or had antiquated and unsafe wiring, none were connected to the sewer system, 34 used wells for water, and 70 had no water. There were six pigpens and numerous chicken and goat pens, and sewage was flowing into Rock Creek. Authorities told owners to pay for upgrades or sell the homes for commercial development. The latter won. The Linden Colored School was located on Garfield Avenue. The Pilgrim Baptist Church and graveyard were located in front of the trees seen above. (Authors' collection.)

www.ingramcontent.com/pod-product-compliance
Lightning Source LLC
Chambersburg PA
CBHW080633110426
42813CB00006B/1673